Maharishi Dayanand Saraswati Book Series- 20

Understanding Pāṇini from Pāṇini's Perspective

A Rebuttal to Cambridge PhD Thesis on Pāṇini

By

Prof. Ravi Prakash Arya
Chair Professor
Maharshi Dayanand Saraswati Chair (UGC)
Maharshi Dayanand University, Rohtak

Rajveer Arya
Research Associate (Hon.)
Maharshi Dayanand Saraswati Chair (UGC)
Maharshi Dayanand University, Rohtak

AMAZON BOOKS, USA
In association with
INDIAN FOUNDATION FOR VEDIC SCIENCE
H.O.1051, Sector-1, Rohtak, Haryana, India
Delhi Contact Ph. Nos.: 09313033917; 09650183260
Emails: vedicscience@gmail.com; vedicscience@rediffmail.com
Website: https://vedic-sciences.com

First Edition

Christian Era: 2023
Vikrama Era: 2080
Kali Era: 5124
Kalpa Era: 1972949124
Brahma Era: 155521972949124

ISBN No. 978-93-94724-13-6

Printed by

Indian Foundation for Vedic Science, 1051, Sector-1, Rohtak-124001, Haryana

Contents

Preface

When Cambridge University awarded a Ph.D. degree on the thesis submitted on Pāṇini to Atul Rishi Raj Popat titled "In Pāṇini We Trust- Discovering the Algorithm for Rule Conflict Resolution in the Aṣṭādhyāyī," it was publicized by Atul Rishi Raj and his supervisor in social, print and mainstream media that 2500-year-old algorithm of Pāṇini has been cracked.

This false and fake propaganda was highly reprimanded and castigated by the Pāṇinian scholars at large in India in social media. Scholars also challenged this false claim. But so far, no documented review of this false propaganda and the Ph.D. thesis has been presented. As such, there was a lot of pressure from many quarters to review this thesis and bring it in a document form for those who want to know the facts about Pāṇini and his machine. Dr. Vivek Arya and Shri Sanjeev Newar were the main force behind this motivation to examine the Ph.D. dissertation submitted to the University of Cambridge.

They cajoled us into deflating the exuberance rife in the media about an ostensible claim of solving 2500-year-old Panini-Vyākaraṇa's Puzzle.

Here it may be clarified that Sanskrit Vyākaraṇa cannot be learned properly through the books like Laghu Siddhānta Kaumudi, etc. These texts present a facet of Sanskrit Vyākaraṇa that appears to be highly impracticable and abstruse. If one wants to learn Sanskrit Vyākaraṇa from a proper perspective, ancient, traditional Ārṣa-vidhi developed by the seers of this land is only the way forward for genuine and serious learners. It will add to the charm of the learner to tread the path which, otherwise, he would not have dared.

The following books are hereby recommended for genuine and serious learners of Sanskrit Vyākaraṇa.

The *Paṭhana Pāṭhana Ki Anubhūta Saralatam Vidhi*-Part-I by Pt. Brahmdutt Jigyasu.

The *Paṭhana Pāṭhana Ki Anubhūta Saralatam Vidhi*-Part-2 by Pt. Yudhishthir Mimanshak.

The *Prathmāvṛtti* on Pāṇini's Vyākaraṇa by Pt Brahmdutt Jigyasu.

The *Prathmāvṛitti* on Pāṇini's Vyākaraṇa by Acharya Sudershan Dev Ji.

The *Vedāṅga Prakāśa* by Maharshi Dayanand.

The *Uṇādi koṣa* by Pt. Yudhishthir Mimanshak.

The *Sanskrit Śikṣaṇa Sarala Saraṇi* by Acharya Ram Shastri.

The *Pāribhāṣika* by Acharya Pradyuman.

It is because of the efforts of these great scholars Ārṣa-vidhi has been resuscitated.

Before presenting this review, let it be clarified that for the convenience of the readers back home, we have used Sanskrit text instead of Roman for Sūtras and Siddhis.

In this treatise, sūtra-numbers have also been assigned based on पाणिनीयः अष्टाध्यायीसूत्रपाठः, compiled by Pt. Brahma Dutta Jigyasu, published by "Shri Ram Lal Kapur Trust, Gurukula Rewali, Sonipat, Haryana, India.

The arrangement of the sūtras is in accordance with Maharshi Patañjali's Mahābhāṣya. Hence, readers are advised not to get confused on seeing the variance in sūtra-numbers with that of the thesis.

The sūtra-numbers in the thesis are based on Kāśikā or Siddhānta Kaumudī; hence, readers are advised to look for the same few numbers prior or later. They will definitely be able to locate the sūtra and will thus be able to verify their numbers by themselves.

Pāribhāṣika readers are advised to refer to Maharshi Dayanand's Vedāṅga Prakāśa-Pāribhāṣikāḥ.

Here it may also be informed that Chapter One of this review is attempted by Prof. Ravi Prakash Arya, and the rest of the chapters are attempted by Rajveer Arya, a student and scholar of Sanskrit Vyākaraṇa associated with Maharshi Dayanand Saraswati Chair (UGC), Maharshi Dayanand University, Rohtak.

Chapter-1

Understanding Pāṇini from Pāṇini's Perspective

Some days back, the thesis of Mr. Rishi Raj Popat titled 'In Pāṇini We Trust- Discovering the Algorithm for Rule Conflict Resolution in the Aṣṭādhyāyī' supervised by Dr. Vincenzo Vergiani, submitted for the degree of Doctor of Philosophy in St. John's College, Faculty of Asian and Middle Eastern Studies, University of Cambridge was doing a round in social, print and mainstream media. It became a very hotly debated issue. Generally, theses submitted in the universities routinely do not draw much attention. They become part of the library shelves. But this thesis was made viral on social and other media sites by Rishi himself, making a tall claim that he has cracked the 2500-year-old algorithm of Pāṇini.

According to the University, leading Sanskrit experts have described Rajpopat's discovery as "revolutionary". The 2,500-year-old algorithm decoded by him makes it possible, for the first time, to accurately use Panini's so-called "language machine". According to the thesis supervisor, Dr. Vincenzo Vergiani, "My student Rishi has cracked it - he has found an extraordinarily elegant solution to a problem which has perplexed scholars for centuries. This discovery will revolutionize the study of Sanskrit at a time when interest in the language is on the rise."

Let me declare at the outset that the algorithm of

Pāṇini was handed down by Pāṇini himself. During the course of time, some doubts emerged which were also resolved by Patañjali in his Mahābhāṣya. This thesis is the glaring proof of pseudo-scholarship. Cambridge is undoubtedly a big name, but the thesis written, supervised, submitted, examined, and accepted is a low-grade one. It is not compatible with the dignity of Cambridge. It will tarnish the image of the University in the eyes of serious scholars of the Pāṇinian system of grammar. Here the student alone cannot be blamed it appears that his supervisor is also oblivious to the intricacies of the Pāṇinian system of grammar, so he blindly allowed it for submission. The examiners, too, are to be blamed. This thesis, as it appears, has been examined by such examiners who, as if, never studied Pāṇini Aṣṭādhyāyī from beginning to end and confined themselves to the teaching and practice of Laghu Siddhānta Kaumudi, etc. The way this petty student is deriding the ancient scholarship, claiming his best understanding of Pāṇini's system of Aṣṭādhyāyi, is not only pitiable but the climax of stupidity in the academic field. Rather I would say it is a big academic blunder. This will be revealed in ensuing discussions.

Despite the widely read and better-known text, Pāṇini's Aṣṭādhyāyī remains a less understood text to date by a good number of scholars. Pāṇini's tradition ends with Munitrayī—three Munis-Pāṇini, Kātyāyana, and Patañjali. In Pāṇini's tradition there is a famous dictum: यथोत्तरं मुनीनां प्रामाण्यम्। Pāṇini, Kātyāyana and Patañjali have their authority one after another. This tradition of Munitrayī ends with Patañjali, and later we find the rise of Prakriyā texts or derivational texts, which were also based upon the Pāṇinian system of grammar.

There is a lot of difference between the Pāṇinian tradition and Post Pāṇinian Prakriyā tradition. Pāṇinian tradition's objective was to provide a grammatical solution, or explanation to the *prayukta* words (words already in use) or the final form of which was already known, whereas the post-Pāṇinian Prakriyā tradition aimed at the derivation of those words, as if they do not know the final forms of words. So, a machine that was used to explain the grammatical structure of the words of which the final form was known, was used to derive the words of which the final form was not actually known or as if not known. It was a 'u-turn' in the Pāṇinian grammatical tradition. Unmindful of this reality, now almost all scholars use the Paṇinian machine as a derivational machine, and several others call it a generative grammar. Thus we find one machine used for two different objectives. We must understand that objective-wise parameters of the same machine will also differ.

To understand Pāṇini from a proper perspective, it is essential to know his actual and factual motive or intention. If we start reading our pre-conceived notions into the text of any author, then we cannot obtain the results as intended by the original author. This is what happened with the post-Pāṇinian derivational schools. In their efforts to derive the unknown words, they had to develop a (vyavasthā), a particular system involving the arrangement of some rules, regulations, and order, etc., by adding some new vārttikas and paribhāṣās to basic formulae of Pāṇini. This student's understanding of Pāṇinian grammar is also the same as those of post-Paṇinian grammarians. Although he questions (p. 15) this post-Pāṇinian understanding as follows:

'But was Pāṇini also aiming to build a somewhat mechanistic model for deriving Sanskrit words (and subsequently, sentences)'? To find the answer to his question, he quotes Kātyāyana's and Patañjali's views about the meaning and purpose of Vyākaraṇa. According to Kātyāyana, 'lakṣyalakṣaṇe vyākaraṇam,' the goal of grammar is to provide rules for words. Similarly, according to Patañjali, vyākaraṇa serves the purposes of rakṣā 'protection of the Vedas by knowing the process of elision', augment and phonemic changes, etc. described by grammar; ūha 'use of gender and case endings as per the requirement of rituals'; āgama 'Śāstras' instruction for the compulsory study of grammar;' laghu 'brevity', i.e., ease of learning the language'; and 'asandeha' resolution of doubts regarding the derivation of words'- *rakṣohāgamalaghvasandehāḥ*.

Herein above, I have not quoted the meaning furnished by the student, but given my interpretation of the words based upon Mahābhāṣya.

However, in the above objectives of grammar explained by both Kātyāyana and Patañjali, he does not find the answer to his question, because he is not able to understand that the above system was not created to give the results intended by him. He is also in the same race as post-Pāṇinian scholars that Pāṇini's grammar has a generative or derivational objective for generating unknown words. This post-Pāṇinian approach may be called extra-Pāṇinian. Any extra-Pāṇinian approach may be partially or maximally based upon the Pāṇinian system but not wholly or in its entirety. The student's approach is also extra-Pāṇinian based upon extrapolation of

Pāṇini's system. Post-Pāṇinian tradition also developed its vyavasthā by extrapolating or intrapolating Pāṇini's basic system through new vārttikas or paribhāṣās. I am not saying that this was wrong. If you want to serve an inverse purpose from the Pāṇini's system that was not basically made for that purpose, naturally, you have to extrapolate or intrapolate his basic system. This extrapolation or intrapolation may be called a new vyavasthā within the original vyavasthā of Pāṇini. But while attempting such extrapolations or intrapolations or developing new vyavasthā within the original vyavasthā of Pāṇini or whosoever he may be, one cannot cross the maryādā (boundary) of language, style, and system developed by the original author. You can do all this within the framework of language, style, and system defined and described by the original author. If you do not want to obey the maryādā established by the original contributor, then you can do so by developing your independent system, which may not be based upon Pāṇini's system without declaring that your un-Pāṇinian system is better than other Pāṇinian systems.

I find the entire post-Pāṇinian tradition to follow the footsteps of Pāṇini while extrapolating or intrapolating his original system. In other words, I can say that their extrapolations or intrapolations are Pāṇinian.

But this student's attempt is quite un-Pāṇinian, although he appears to make a tall claim that he was able to solve a 2500-year-old problem which was, in reality, never a problem. His understanding of Pāṇini and his system is naïve and childish. I am not against his attempt, there must be attempts to understand the system from different perspectives, but while understanding a system from a different perspective, we cannot disobey the principles or guidelines set by the system. We should understand any concerned system within its framework. The present student is not attempting to extrapolate or intrapolate Pāṇini's system within Pāṇini's framework or guidelines, but disregarding his system and guidelines, sometimes misrepresenting him and sometimes forcing his own views on him to prove his failed attempt successful. This will be clear in the discussions that will follow.

First of all, we must not forget that grammar is always developed to explain the existing material. After the grammar had been developed, it may regularise the future and further use of words keeping them in its four corners. But Pāṇini developed such a magnificent mechanistic model that could not only explain the grammatical structure of the words known to him (current in the Vedas and Loka), but it could also derive unknown words or generate new words. As such, his grammar also became famous as generative grammar.

This mechanistic generative model was first reviewed by Āchārya Kātyāyana when he dealt with the issue of mutual opposition of sūtras and order of rule applied to explain the grammatical structure of the words unknown to Pāṇini or missed by him with the help of Pāṇinian system of grammar. This is evident from the following vārttika in the context of Pāṇini's most debated sūtra: विप्रतिषेधे परं कार्यम् 1.4.2.

गुणवृद्ध्यौत्वतृज्वद्भावेभ्यो नुम्पूर्वविप्रतिषिद्धम्। (1) on Pāṇ. 7.1.95

नुमचिरतृज्वद्भावेभ्यो नुट् इति। (2) on Pāṇ. 7.1.95

guṇavṛddhyautvatṛjvadbhāvebhyo

numpūrvavipratiṣiddham (1)
numachiratṛjvad-bhāvebhyo nuṭ iti (2)

In the above vārttikas and similar other vārttikas, Kātyāyana talks about pūrva-pratiṣedha where para-pratiṣedha is not applicable. This shows that he was not able to explain the grammatical structure of certain words based upon the 'later in series' interpretation of the term 'para' written in the sūtra 1.4.2 of Aṣṭādhyāyī, which was primarily intended by Pāṇini.

This issue is clarified by Patañjali while dealing with the application of विप्रतिषेध in Pāṇini sūtra 1.4.2. Accordingly,

यथान्यासमेवास्तु । कथं ये पूर्वविप्रतिषेधाः ? विप्रतिषेधे परमित्येव सिद्धम् । कथम् ? परशब्दोऽयं बह्वर्थः । अस्त्येव व्यवस्थायां वर्तते । तद्यथा - पूर्वः परः इति। अस्त्यन्यार्थे वर्तते - परपुत्रः परभार्या अन्यपुत्रः अन्यभार्येति गम्यते । अस्ति प्राधान्ये वर्त्तते । तद्यथा - परमियं ब्राह्मण्यस्मिन्कुटुम्बे प्रधानमिति गम्यते । अस्तीष्टवाची परशब्दः । तद्यथा - परं धाम गतः इष्टं धामेति गम्यते । तद्य इष्टवाची परशब्दस्तस्येदं ग्रहणं विप्रतिषेधे परं यदिष्टं तद्भवतीति ।

yathānyāsamevāstu / katham ye pūrvavipratiṣedhāḥ ? vipratiṣedhe paramityeva siddham / katham ? paraśabdo'yaṁ bahvarthaḥ / astyeva vyavasthāyāṁ vartate / tadyathā - pūrvaḥ paraḥ iti / astyanyārthe vartate - paraputraḥ parabhāryā anyaputraḥ anyabhāryeti gamyate / asti prādhānye varttate / tadyathā - paramiyaṁ brāhmaṇyasminkuṭumbe pradhānamiti gamyate / astīṣṭavāchī paraśabdaḥ / tadyathā - paraṁ dhāma gataḥ iṣṭaṁ dhāmeti gamyate / tadya iṣṭavāchī paraśabdastasyedaṁ grahaṇaṁ vipratiṣedhe paraṁ yadiṣṭaṁ tadbhavatīti /

[Meaning] Let this sūtra be retained as it was read by Āchārya Pāṇini, i.e. विप्रतिषेधे परं कार्यम् 1.4.2. If we retain this sūtra as it is, how can pūrva-pratiṣedha operation take place? Answer is, through sūtra विप्रतिषेधे परं कार्यम् 1.4.2. pūrva-pratiṣedha operations will also be accomplished. How? The word 'para' used in the sūtra has multi-meanings. Firstly it signifies vyavasthā (arrangement, or order of placement), e.g., pūrva (east or left side in horizontal order of placement), para (west or right side in horizontal order placement); pūrva (north or above in vertical placement), para (south or below in vertical placement). Secondly, it signifies 'other,' e.g., para-putra (other's son), para-bhāryā (other's wife). Thirdly, 'para' is used to signify 'headship, dominance, powerfulness or superiority,' e.g., 'this lady is (param) head of this family. Para also signifies 'desired one', e.g., she went to (param dhāma) her desired abode. So, here in विप्रतिषेध (vipratiṣedha) 'para' word signifies iṣṭa (desired), i.e., 'application of the rule that gives us 'desired result'.

From the aforementioned discussion of Mahābhāṣya, it is crystal clear that according to Mahābhāṣyakāra Patañjali, the word 'param' in sūtra विप्रतिषेधे परं कार्यम् 1.4.2 stands for 'desired', kārya कार्य stands for both 'operation' and 'effect or result' and vipratiṣedha विप्रतिषेध stands for 'mutual opposition'. As such, the complete meaning of the sūtra, as per Mahābhāṣyakāra, is 'in the matter of mutual opposition of sūtras, the sūtra that can give desired result should be applied'. In other words, in the matter of mutual opposition of sūtras, that sūtra will operate, which will give us the desired result.

Mahābhāṣyakāra clearly understood the motive of Pāṇini's work which was the explanation of the grammatical structure of the prayukta words (whose final form was known to the Āchārya). That is why, Patañjali pointed out that the term 'param kāryam' in the sūtra विप्रतिषेधे परं कार्यम् means "*yad iṣṭam tad bhavati*", i.e. that sūtra will apply which can give the desired result'.

Thus we can see that so far as prayukta words (of which the final form is known) are concerned, we can derive them with the help of suitable sūtra giving the iṣṭa (desired) effect or result. This is the real understanding of Pāṇini's sūtra. As such the tall claims both by the student and his teacher that they have cracked the 2500-year-old algorithm of Pāṇini and leading Sanskrit experts branding of the student's discovery as "revolutionary" is both shallow and hollow. There was nothing to be cracked in this algorithm.

For instance, we come across that the verbal form 'tudati' from root √tud+ tip (suffix) is in currency. While explaining the grammatical structure of 'tudati', we come across Pāṇini's sūtra पुगन्तलघूपधस्य च-7.3.86, which suggests guṇa replacement of 'u' in √tud and तुदादिभ्यः शः -3.1.77 suggesting the insertion of 'śa' infix (vikaraṇa) between √tud+ tip> √tud+śa+tip. Here given the known form tudati, even a beginner of Pāṇinian school can easily decide that in this case तुदादिभ्यः शः -3.1.77 will be applicable and not पुगन्तलघूपधस्य च-7.3.86, because if he applies पुगन्तलघूपधस्य च-7.3.86, the resulting form would be 'todati' which is not the current form, and suppose 'todati' is current, then पुगन्तलघूपधस्य च-7.3.86 will become applicable.

This efficiency of Pāṇini's machine in explaining the grammatical structure, which is the basic motive of the Āchārya cannot be doubted when 'param kāryam' in विप्रतिषेधे परं कार्यम् is understood properly in terms of Patañjali.

Yes, if we want to serve the different purpose which is being attempted in post-Pāṇinian tradition, i.e., deriving the unknown words or generating new worlds, the above interpretation of 'param kāryam' will no longer work. In this regard, the term 'param kāryam' in विप्रतिषेधे परं कार्यम् will have to be interpreted differently and that different meaning has also been suggested by Patañjali himself as: अस्त्येव व्यवस्थायां वर्तते । तद्यथा - पूर्वः परः इति, i.e. 'pūrva' and 'param' also signifies vyavasthā.

Here, we should know what is vyavasthā? Vyavasthā, here, means an arrangement, order of placement. This arrangement or order may be in terms of space or time. This arrangement or order in terms of space can also be called horizontal placement/ arrangement. Arrangement or order in terms of time can be called vertical placement. Spatial or temporal arrangements are always relative.

For example, in temporal or chronological arrangement or vertical arrangement, pūrva means prior or first in terms of time, and para means later in terms of time. A person born in 1956 will be 'pūrva' relative to a person born in 1960, and a person born in 1960 will be 'pūrva' relative to a person born in 1964. Similarly, a person born in 1964 will be 'para' relative to a person born in 1960.

In spatial arrangement or horizontal placement, 'pūrva' means first in horizontal order, which may also be called east, north, or left, and 'para' means second in horizontal order which may also be called west or south or right. When we shall use the word vyavasthā in the context of Pāṇini's Aṣṭādhyāyī, it will be in terms of spatial, i.e. horizontal placement. When two operating rules or operands are placed horizontally, the first one will be called 'pūrva', and the second one will be called 'para .' Pāṇini is a seer; he has followed natural laws in his Śāstra. He dissected all words into four constituents called prakṛti (base word), vikaraṇa (infix), āgama (augment) and pratyaya (suffix). As such in the spatial or horizontal placement of prakṛti (base word) + pratyaya, prakṛti is pūrva and pratyaya is para. That is why he declares प्रत्ययः (Pāṇ. 3.1.1) परश्च (Pāṇ. 3.1.2). This clearly means that when pratyaya will be spatially or horizontally placed with prakṛti, they will be treated as a para with respect to prakṛti and prakṛti will be treated pūrva with respect to pratyaya. Similarly, Pāṇini's sūtra placement also comes in the domain of spatial or horizontal placement. As per this rule, the first sūtra in order will be considered as 'pūrva' relative to the next sūtra in order, and the next sūtra in order will be considered as 'para' relative to the first sūtra in order. In the Pāṇinian system of grammar and in the sūtra विप्रतिषेधे परं कार्यम्, when the term 'para' signifies 'vyavasthā', it will include both types of placements—placement of sūtras and placement of operands (prakṛti, pratyaya, etc.). Patañjali, in delineating the term vyavasthā has not restricted its meaning to a particular placement. So, in context of vyavasthā, in respect of the sūtra विप्रतिषेधे परं कार्यम्, 'param kāryam' may have two meanings:

1. Sūtra occurring next in the series, will operate.

2. Sūtra applying to para operand (i.e., pratyaya)' will operate

All post-Pāṇinian grammatical tradition followed the meaning 'vyavasthā' drawn through the first meaning of 'para' suggested by Patañjali while supplementing or complementing Pāṇini's basic rules with new paribhāṣās (metarules) or vārttikas (additional rules, amendment rules or supplementary rules). It also appears that while following the vyavasthā, the term 'para' suggested by Patañjali was taken for the first sense drawn from vyavasthā, i.e., sūtra occurring next in the series will operate.

On the basis of 'prādhānya' meaning of 'para'; paribhāṣās signifying 'balatva' 'abalatva', 'pūrva-pratiṣedha', 'para-pratiṣedha', etc. were made.

This student's interpretation of 'para' as the Right-hand side is part of the meaning 'vyavasthā' drawn from the second meaning of 'param' suggested by Patañjali himself.

LHS & RHS Operands

So, the student's insistence is that in the Pāṇini's sūtra विप्रतिषेधे परं कार्यम्, the term 'paraṁ kāryam' does not mean "operation of next sūtra in series" but the operation on RHS operand.

Thus the main contribution of the student is presenting an alternative to the traditional solution by his mechanism of solving the same by operation on RHS operand. Let me observe that concept of operation on LHS and RHS is not Pāṇinian. It is a childish concept. It's not a language of grammar either. What to say of Pāṇini, no neo and naïve grammarian will also use it. It appears that the student has captured these right and left terms from Roodbergen (1991:313), as Roodbergen translates the word 'pūrvāpara' as left-to-right. Accordingly, "The word building process proceeds in what is visually a left-to-right direction'. According to him, this direction of word-building which underlies the functioning of the Aṣṭādhyāyī, impacts its structure, that is, the positioning of rules in different books and chapters of the Aṣṭādhyāyī. Rules dealing with left-side elements are introduced earlier than rules dealing with right-side elements'.

Here, the evidence is clear that the student has captured RHS and LHS concepts from Roodbergen; although Roodbergen did not use these words in the same sense, they are used by the student.

Moreover, the term 'para kārya' in the given sūtra cannot stand for "RHS operation" so far as Pāṇini's language is concerned. Yes, no doubt in the spatial placement of things, "para" also means "right", as discussed above. Instead of using RHS, had the student used "para" for "pratyaya (suffix) operand, which is also placed next (right-hand side) to prakṛti in spatial or horizontal placement, I would have appreciated it to some extent, as this term is within the jurisdiction of Pāṇinian language. Whatever he wants to show as RHS operations, most of such operations are taking place on pratyayas (suffixes) when prakṛti and pratyaya are juxtaposed together. Here the main point to be noticed is that the term 'para' is related to the term 'vipratiṣedha'. In the case of 'vipratiṣedha' between two (one of them is pūrva and another is para), whether the operation will be on para (student), or operation of para (tradition) will take place. Here, it is very important to know the meaning of 'vipratiṣedha'. We find many meanings assigned to 'vipratiṣedha' by different texts and scholars. Most western scholars take 'vipratiṣedha' to mean 'rule conflict'. Kāśikā takes is to mean 'tulyabala-virodha'.

Mahābhāṣya and Maharshi Dayanand Saraswati take it to mean "mutual opposition or mutual blocking". The same meaning is accepted by the student. However, the difference between student and tradition is that according to tradition, the mutual opposition is between two rules, and according to the student, the mutual opposition is between two operands. But there should be some ground for mutual opposition. Without a ground, there can be no opposition. So, in the case of rules, the ground for their mutual opposition is their different purposes or objectives. This issue has been highlighted in the Mahābhāṣya and Maharshi Dayanand Saraswati in his Aṣṭādhyāyī Bhāṣya as:

द्वौ प्रसङ्गौ यदान्यार्थौ भवत एकस्मिंश्च युगपत्प्राप्नुतः स विप्रतिषेधः

dvau prasaṅgau yadānyārthau bhavata ēkasmiṁścha yugapatprāpnutaḥ sa vipratiṣedhaḥ

[Meaning] Vipratiṣedha is simultaneous application of two rules with different objectives at one place or item.

The opposition between two rules with different motives can be understood. Similarly, for the opposition between two operands, there should be some ground. Without a ground, the opposition between the two operands is not understandable. Can the student explain this opposition between two RHS and LHS operands? Why should they oppose each other? Opposition between two operands is totally an absurd idea and so is the interpretation. Let me tell you that western scholars' interpretation of vipratiṣedha as "rule conflict" is far better than that of the student's opposition between two operands. The student is trying to rise above Patañjali, so he should be ready to give justifications for his speculations. This issue has been discussed in detail, while the meaning of vipratiṣedha will be discussed.

Here it may also be pointed out that while presenting his alternate mechanism of derivation, he cannot deride the mechanism discovered by post-Paṇinian tradition, as post-Pāṇinian tradition has always worked in the four corners of Pāṇini's principles and never crossed the maryādā. Moreover, post-Pāṇinian tradition has presented foolproof solutions to all derivational problems. To date, we have not found even a single word that could not be derived based on post-Pāṇinian tradition. Their understanding of the Pāṇinian system is much better than that of the student. Moreover, when you are suggesting an alternative mechanism, you cannot declare your mechanism as the superior one and start deriding others. You conjectured a mechanism that can apply to only a couple of cases, not all. There are more exceptions than solutions in your mechanism.

Linear reading of Aṣṭādhyāyī

Here, we have one more moot point. Scholars have many misconceptions about Pāṇini and Patañjali. Our student says that Bronkhorst (2004) opines that Patañjali prefers a linear reading of Aṣṭādhyāyī. After a long discussion, our student concludes (p. 19) that Pāṇini did intend for the Aṣṭādhyāyī to be interpreted linearly and as a closed grammatical machine. I agree with the conclusion of the student to the extent that Pāṇini intended Aṣṭādhyāyī to be interpreted linearly, but Pāṇini did not intend linear reading of Aṣṭādhyāyī for derivational purposes. Linear reading is limited only to the interpretation of Aṣṭādhyāyī.

Wrong Translation of *Kāśikā vṛtti* on sūtra 1.4.2.

On sūtra 1.4.2 Kāśikā comments as follows:

तुल्यबलविरोधो विप्रतिषेधः। यत्र द्वौ प्रसङ्गावन्यार्थवेकस्मिन् युगपत् प्राप्नुतः, स तुल्यबलविरोधो विप्रतिषेधः। तस्मिन् विप्रतिषेधे परं कार्यं भवति। उत्सर्गापवादनित्यानित्यान्तरङ्गबहिरङ्गेषु तुल्यबलता न अस्तीति न अयमस्य योगस्य विषयः। बलवतैव तत्र भवितव्यम्। अप्रवृत्तौ, पर्यायेण वा प्रवृत्तौ प्राप्तायां वचनमारभ्यते। अतो दीर्घो यञि ७.३.१०१, सुपि च ७.३.१०२ इत्यस्य अवकाशः वृक्षाभ्याम्, प्लक्षाभ्याम्। बहुवचने झल्येत् ७.३.१०३ इत्यस्य अवकाशः वृक्षेषु, प्लक्षेषु। इह उभयं प्राप्नोति वृक्षेभ्यः, प्लक्षेभ्यः इति। परं भवति विप्रतिषेधेन।

tulyabalavirodho vipratiṣedhaḥ। yatra dvau prasaṅgāvanyārthavekasmin yugapat prāpnutaḥ, sa tulyabalavirodho vipratiṣedhaḥ। tasmin vipratiṣedhe paraṁ kāryaṁ bhavati। utsargāpavādanityānityāntaraṅgabahiraṅgeṣu tulyabalatā na astīti na ayamasya yogasya viṣayaḥ। balavataiva tatra bhavitavyam। apravṛttau, paryāyeṇa vā pravṛttau prāptāyāṁ vachanamārabhyate। ato dīrgho yañi 7.3.101, supi cha 7.3.102 ityasya avakāśaḥ vṛkṣābhyām, plakṣābhyām। bahuvachane jhalyet 7.3.103 ityasya avakāśaḥ vṛkṣeṣu, plakṣeṣu। iha ubhayaṁ prāpnoti vṛkṣebhyaḥ, plakṣebhyaḥ iti। paraṁ bhavati vipratiṣedhena।

The student translates the above passage of Kāśikā in the name of tradition as under:

> 'The word vipratiṣedha means "conflict." When two operations that can be applied at other sites become simultaneously applicable at one [and the same site], this is called a conflict of equal strength or vipratiṣedha. In the event of vipratiṣedha, the

rule that comes later [in the serial order of the Aṣṭādhyāyī] prevails. A general rule (utsarga) and its exception (apavāda), or a nitya rule and an anitya rule, or an antaraṅga and a bahiraṅga rule, are not rules of equal strength. These pairs do not fall under the jurisdiction of this rule. In these cases, the stronger rule wins. When both rules are unable to apply, or when they are only able to apply alternatively, this rule comes into play.'

Our student is confused and wrongly interprets the following sentence of Kāśikā-यत्र द्वौ प्रसङ्गावन्यार्थवेकस्मिन् युगपत् प्राप्नुतः. He interprets it as: 'When two operations which can be applied at other sites become simultaneously applicable at one [and the same site].'

He is not able to understand the term प्रसङ्गावन्यार्थौ. Here, it means 'when two rules with different objectives/purposes/motives apply simultaneously at one and the same place.' For example, in the case of vṛkṣa+bhyaḥ, the rules अतो दीर्घो यञि 7.3.101 suggests the lengthening the short vowel of vṛkṣa 'a' into 'ā,' but the rule बहुवचने झल्येत् 7.3.103 suggests the substitution of 'a-final' of vṛkṣa to 'e.' Thus, in this case, two different rules with different objectives- one with the objective of lengthening the short vowel 'a' and another with the objective of substituting 'a' with 'e'- apply at the one and same 'a' of vṛkṣa.

On the other hand, our student has no understanding of प्रसङ्गावन्यार्थौ. According to him, 'anyārthau' means 'two operations which can be applied at other sites.' This is wrong. That is why, due to this misunderstanding of the 'anyārthau', he interprets vipratiṣedha as 'opposition between two operands.' His whole hypothesis is standing on this false conjecture, so destined to collapse. The correct meaning is 'two rules with different motives.' He would not have made this castle in the air if he had known the correct meaning. It shows that the student is playing with the fire of Pāṇini's grammar, and the supervisors and examiners are oblivious to it, being unable to understand Kāśikā vṛtti of Aṣṭādhyāyī. It is a sad situation and a height of academic stupidity. If you are not able to understand the meaning of one simple sentence, how can you understand the complex system of Pāṇini's Aṣṭādhyāyī, which is fraught with complex codes?

Alternate version of विप्रतिषेधे परं कार्यम् (1.4.2) and कडारादेका संज्ञा (1.4.1) in Mahābhāṣya

After suggesting the wrong interpretation of Kāśikā-Vṛtti on Pāṇini 1.4.2, our student has come out with the alternate versions of the sūtras under reference above quoted in Mahābhāṣya (pp. 28-29). First of all, he should know the objective of the author of Mahābhāṣya. It is said:

शंका समाधान परो ग्रन्थो भाष्यम्।

śaṁkā samādhāna paro grantho bhāṣyam

[Meaning] That is bhāṣya is a text that deals with the doubts and their solutions with regard to the interpretation of the Aṣṭādhyāyī of Pāṇini.

Patañjali, while writing his Mahābhāṣya on Aṣṭādhyāyī, did not want to leave even a single question unanswered raised by scholars after the death of Pāṇini till his time. On विप्रतिषेधे परं कार्यम् sūtra, he resolved the doubts raised during those days. It was doubted that had

विप्रतिषेधे परम् version of the sūtra solved the problem, why Pāṇini would have suggested a bigger version विप्रतिषेधे परं कार्यम्, as the brevity was considered the beauty of the sūtras. There was a saying that if a grammarian is able to reduce half mora (mātrā) from a sūtra, he celebrates it like the birth of a child. अर्धमात्रा लाघवेन पुत्रोत्सवं मन्यन्ते वैयाकरणाः। Discussing all pros and cons related with both the versions विप्रतिषेधे परं and विप्रतिषेधे परं कार्यम्, Patañjali finally resolves the issue saying यथान्यासमेवास्तु, i.e. the original reading of the Āchārya विप्रतिषेधे परं कार्यम् is appropriate and so be retained.

Similarly, there is mention of two versions of आ कडारादेका संज्ञा and प्राक् कडारात् परं कार्यम् being taught by Pāṇini to his students. In the Mahābhāṣya, a huge discussion has followed from different angles on the veracity of two different versions. The first version of 1.4.1 says that each item can take only one sañjñā, i.e. each item can have only one technical nomenclature up to 2.2.38- *kadārā karmadhārye* and the second version of 1.4.1 says that prior to *kadārā* (2.2.38) only succeeding rule will operate. Here it should be known that if the first version of 1.4.1 आ कडारादेका संज्ञा goes with first version of 1.4.2 विप्रतिषेधे परं कार्यम् and second version of 1.4.1 प्राक् कडारात् परं कार्यम् goes with the second version of 1.4.2. विप्रतिषेधे परं, no operation will be basically affected. For example, in the word rakṣa रक्ष, a-final of 'ra' takes 'laghu' sañjñā by the rule ह्रस्वं लघु (1.4.10) and the same 'a' takes guru sañjñā by virtue of the sūtra संयोगे गुरु (1.4.11). If we go by the first version of 1.4.1 आ कडारादेका संज्ञा, it would suggest that 'a' can take only one sañjñā and the first version of sūtra 1.4.2 विप्रतिषेधे परं कार्यम् will decide that para-sūtra 1.4.11 will operate instead of pūrva sūtra 1.4.10, between two sūtras operating simultaneously at one place, i.e., 'a' with different motives. If we go by the second version of 1.4.1 प्राक् कडारात् परं कार्यम् and 1.4.2 विप्रतिषेधे परं, then also 'a-final' of the word 'rakṣa रक्ष', will take take guru sañjñā by virtue of para sūtra संयोगे गुरु (1.4.11). So, both versions if applied correspondingly, there will be no change in the result.

Our student could not understand this mystery. He makes surmises and says, "That while the two versions of 1.4.1 say different things (one says *ekā saṁjñā* and the other says *paraṁ kāryam*), the two versions of 1.4.2 essentially say the same thing. So, what does the alternative version of 1.4.1, i.e., *prāk kaḍārāt paraṁ kāryam* exactly, mean? It translates as, between 1.4.1 and 2.2.38, the latter rule should be applied. But when? In which context or situation? This version of 1.4.1 is, at best ambiguous. Secondly, it seems very unlikely that Pāṇini would teach two different versions of his own rules to his pupils. In the following chapter, I reinterpret the meaning of para, which makes it clear that the alternate version of 1.4.1 does not make sense. For all these reasons, I conclusively reject the alternate version." (p. 29)

He himself is not able to understand the fact that both versions of sūtra 1.4.1 and 1.4.2 will go together respectively to give the same result, and he rejects the alternate versions and reinterpret the meaning of 'para'. Here, both Sanskrit and Hindi sayings are exactly applicable:

नैष स्थाणोरपराधो यदेनमन्धो न पश्यति ।

naiṣa sthāṇoraparādho yadenamandho na paśyati ।

[Meaning] It is not the mistake of a pillar if a blind

person is not able to see it.

बिल्ली को अंगुर नहीं मिले तो अंगुर खट्टे।

billī ko aṁgura nahīṁ mile to aṁgura khaṭṭe ।

[Meaning] Grapes are sour if the cat fails to access them.

So far, his refutation of Kiparsky is concerned (p. 29); he is right. The scope of 1.4.2 is not restricted to 2.2.38, but it applies to the entire Aṣṭādhyāyī.

SSRI/DOI/SOI

Based upon a wrong interpretation of द्वौ प्रसङ्गौ यदान्यार्थौ भवत एकस्मिंश्च युगपत्प्राप्नुतः स विप्रतिषेधः quoted in Kāśikā-vṛtti on Pāṇini 1.4.2, as already discussed above, the student has conjectured some new concepts like SSRI (same step rule interaction), DOI (different operand interaction), and SOI (same operand interaction), which is un-Pāṇinian at the very outset. He wants to test the application of Pāṇini's rule 1.4.2 to his conjectured concepts built upon the wrong translation of Kāśikā. To make Pāṇini's rule applicable to his concept, the traditional application is not going to help him, so he brands traditional interpretation as misinterpretation. As per his own interpretation, Pāṇinian rule deals with competition between two operands and not two rules. In his hypothesis built upon wrong interpretations, he has miserably failed to justify and explain why there is competition between two operands. Moreover, he himself accepts that his interpretation does not hold true in all cases of SOI and DOI. It holds true in cases of DOI, so he had to remark (p. 39) that Pāṇini has not given any instruction about SOI but taught the metarule 1.4.2 for dealing with DOI.

This is the height of an academic blunder. He has conjectured some new concepts and tries to verify his conjectured concepts in the light of Pāṇini's rule, but when he fails to do so, instead of coming to the right conclusion that his conjectured concept of DOI and SOI is not in consonance with Pāṇinian rule, he blames Pāṇini that he did not give any instruction about SOI. Pāṇini did not have a dream that some student in Cambridge would try to read his grammar to verify his stipulated equation of SOI, so he failed to give instructions to deal with his concept of SOI. In fact, Pāṇini does not intend what this student expects from him. He wants to put his words into the mouth of Pāṇini. This also proves that the student's claim of the right understanding of Pāṇinian rule is a hoax.

Moreover, the concepts of DOI and SOI are basically wrong. The words of the Sanskrit language were not made by combining base+infix+augment+suffix, etc., as speculated by the student. These were found to be used by the seers in their final forms. So, they attempted to analyze their grammatical structure by dissecting or splitting them into bases+infixes+augments+suffixes, etc. Vyākaraṇa itself means analysis. For this student, these are all separate items, but for Pāṇini, these are part of one single-word family split into various constituents. Pāṇini made a rule not to deal with them as separate items placed as left or right as the student thinks, rather he made rules in view of these various constituents qualified to be operands as per their sañjñās, i.e. nomenclatures. Perhaps, the student is not aware of the beauty of the Pāṇinian system, so he discards the system of sañjñā-karaṇa and says that there cannot be more than one sañjñā and there is no need of sañjñā-karaṇa (giving a name) to an infix. Pāṇinian system ceases to work for want of sañjñās. For any qualified operation, the operand should be designated with a sañjñā. As such, operation on an operand designated with some sañjñā will take precedence over any other operation involving a varṇa, i.e. an operand without designation. That is why a vārttika was made in Paribhāṣenduśekhara: वार्णादाङ्गं बलीयो भवति Paribhāṣā 55.

The student further claims, "We can say that Pāṇini has given explicit instructions about how we must deal with competition between operands (which we see in DOI but not in SOI), but not about how we must deal with competition between rules (which we see in both DOI and SOI)."

As pointed out above, wishful thinking of the student that Pāṇini has given explicit instructions about how we must deal with competition between operands is based upon his wrong interpretation of Kāśikā-vṛtti on Pāṇ. 1.4.2. In Kāśikā, it is mentioned

यत्र द्वौ प्रसङ्गावन्यार्थवेकस्मिन् युगपत् प्राप्नुतः।

yatra dvau prasaṅgāvanyārthavekasmin yugapat prāpnutaḥ ।

But the student wrongly interprets it as: 'When two operations which can be applied at other sites become simultaneously applicable at one [and the same site].'

He is not able to understand the meaning of the phrase प्रसङ्गावन्यार्थौ, which means 'when two rules with different objectives/purposes/motives simultaneously apply at one and the same place'.

If we follow the above given right interpretation of

Kāśikā, then we shall find, contrary to the view of the student, that Pāṇini has given explicit instructions about how we must deal with competition between two rules operating with different objectives.

Aṅgādhikāra

Aṅgādhikāra forms part of the fourth chapter (4.1) of the thesis of the student. There he discusses in detail the Pāṇini sūtra यस्मात् प्रत्ययविधिस्तदादि प्रत्ययेऽङ्गम् 1.4.13. He says that he does not approve of the traditional interpretation of the sūtra, and so prefers to interpret this sūtra in his own way suitable to his conjectures. His problem is that he has not learned Aṣṭādhyāyī from an expert teacher. His arguments and criticism are based on the English translations. More often than not, English translators, as I have seen, do not have deep knowledge of the Śāstras, but they start translating them because they have a good command over writing English. Not only Pāṇini's grammar but most of the Sanskrit works also face this music by default. The reader is always at the receiving end.

To start with the above sūtra, let me first give the exact translation of the sūtra, which is as under:

'When a प्रत्यय is attached to a dhātu (verbal base) or prātipadika (nominal base), everything that begins with the first letter of that dhātu or prātipadika up to (and excluding) the first letter of the प्रत्ययः itself, is designated an अङ्ग of that प्रत्यय. Here vikaraṇa, along with a base, and augment is also designated as अङ्ग.'

Now I quote the translation of Sharma referred to by the student in his thesis (4.1, p. 109). It reads as: 'a form beginning with that after which an affix is introduced is termed aṅga when the affix follows.'

Literal translation is correct, but it gives one nothing to understand. In fact, the translator himself appears to be aloof from what Pāṇini intends to say. Not only this, the English translation of S.C. Vasu is worthy to be noted. He translates as under:

'After whatsoever there is an affix enjoined, whether verbal or crude-form, that which begins therewith in the form in which it appears when the affix follows it, is called an अङ्ग 'Inflective base'.

S.C. Vasu is translating aṅga as the inflective base, which is wrong. Aṅga is already a technical term or nomenclature used by Pāṇini; if we translate the technical terms or nomenclature, the very purpose of doing 'sañjñā' will be marred.

If any student or his teacher brushes up his knowledge based upon such vague translations, they will certainly remain in confusion and cannot learn anything except criticizing the original author and befooling themselves and confusing others. They will always remain oblivious to the technicalities and beauties of Sanskrit Śāstras.

Patañjali has given the purpose of 'tadādi' word in the sūtra quoting a vārttika as:

अथ तदादिग्रहणं किमर्थम् ? अङ्गसंज्ञायां तदादिग्रहणं स्यादिनुमर्थम् ॥ १ ॥ अङ्गसंज्ञायां तदादिग्रहणं क्रियते स्याद्यर्थं नुमर्थं च ।

atha tadādigrahaṇaṁ kimartham ? aṅgasaṁjñāyāṁ tadādigrahaṇaṁ syādinumartham // 1 // aṅgasaṁjñāyāṁ tadādigrahaṇaṁ kriyate syādyarthaṁ numarthaṁ cha /

[Meaning] What is the purpose of mentioning

tadādi in the sūtra? He says that 'tadādi' word has been used so that the (sya) infix or vikaraṇa and (num) augment may also be included in the jurisdiction of aṅga sañjñā of pratyaya along with their base.

Since the student does not know the actual meaning of the sūtra, so he insists that only one item, in his opinion, can be called an aṅga with respect to a certain pratyaya in a derivation (p. 109). His problem is that he wants to 'trust Pāṇini', but he does not have the right translations to maintain his trust in Pāṇini. As a result, his trust keeps on wavering, which is reflected sometimes by his wrong translations of the sūtras and others by not following the intended sense of the sūtras. He does not know the fact that initially, vikaraṇa, āgamas and pratyayas are the part or members of the same family called a word, which were analyzed by the Vaiyākaraṇas. Now, with the commencement of the reverse order of deriving words, these separated vikaraṇas, āgamas and pratyayas are going to be united with their family again. For being united, they shall have to be given suitable designation so that they may accept operations per their designation as it may help them unite with their family again. So, Pāṇini is making rules by considering them as one family. As such, in the case of chit+śap, when a vikaraṇa (śap) combines with its base (chit), both will be the aṅga of pratyaya (tip), being the member of one and the same family. Sanskrit is a natural language. So, it requires natural rules to regulate its forms and not artificial regulations.

But this student is obsessed with giving a new interpretation to the rules because he found the interpretation of 'tadādi' missing from Sharma's vague translation which he calls a traditional interpretation. Now we shall analyze his own interpretation. He interprets the rule (p. 110-111) as under:

> 'Upon the addition of pratyaya (tip) to base (chit), that which begins with base (chit) is called aṅga when pratyaya (tip) follows.'

His translation is worst than Mr. Sharma's (quoted by him). Mr. Sharma did the translation of 'tadādi', but it was vague, because he could not understand the purpose of its use in the sūtra. Let us see what does the student observe?

> 'Let us first look at chit. If Pāṇini wanted us to treat chit as an aṅga with respect to tiP, he could have simply said *yasmāt pratyayavidhis tad pratyaye'ṅgam* 'a form after which an affix is introduced is termed aṅga when the affix follows.' Thus, I do not think that we should call chit an aṅga with respect to tiP. This leaves us with two options: chit + ŚaP and cheta. Let us closely consider 1.4.13 in the context of this derivation to decide which of the two should be called an aṅga with respect to tiP.
>
> *yasmāt* – to (lit. after) chit
>
> *pratyayavidhis* – (upon addition of tiP)
>
> ***tadādi* – that which begins with chit**
>
> *pratyaye* – when tiP follows
>
> *aṅgam* – (is called) aṅga.
>
> 'Upon the addition of tiP to chit, that which begins with chit is called aṅga when tiP follows.'

He further observes, 'The form which begins with chit is an aṅga with respect to tiP. Can we say that chit + ŚaP begins with chit? I do not think so. I think chit + ŚaP is still just a string of two separate items, namely the root chit and the vikaraṇa affix ŚaP. Only when they are fused into a single form that begins with chit that form can be called an aṅga with respect to tiP. When can we fuse chit and ŚaP into a single form? I think we can do that after applying all possible rules to chit and ŚaP, except those that are triggered by tiP.'

In the above observation, he is in confusion when he translates 'tadādi' as 'that which begins with chit'. But the correct meaning of tadādi is 'from the beginning letter of chit dhātu till the initial letter of tip. As such, this 'tadādi' term covers everything sandwiched between the initial letter of dhātu/prātipadika (chit) and the initial letter of pratyaya (tip).

Due to this wrong understanding of the sūtra, he is ready to demolish everything. In his first attempt, he discards the 'chit' being aṅga of 'tip.' In his second attempt, he discards the combination of chit+ śap, saying that in his opinion, cit + ŚaP does not begin with cit? as cit + ŚaP is still just a string of two separate items, namely the root chit and the vikaraṇa affix ŚaP. But he fails to understand that chit+śap is not the string of two separate items; rather, they are the member of one family (word) separated to understand the construction of that word.

This shows that the basic meanings and fundamentals of Pāṇini's grammar are not clear to this student, and he is all out to attack scholars like Patañjali and feed his words to the mouth of Pāṇini.

Interpretation of Vipratiṣedha

Vipratiṣedha is defined by Mahābhāṣyakāra as:

विप्रतिषेध इति कोऽयं शब्दः ? विप्रतिपूर्वात्सिधेः कर्मव्यतिहारे घञ् । इतरेतरप्रतिषेधो विप्रतिषेधः । अन्योन्यप्रतिषेधो विप्रतिषेधः ।

vipratiṣedha iti ko'yaṁ śabdaḥ ? vipratipūrvātsidheḥ karmavyatihāre ghañ । itaretarapratiṣedho vipratiṣedhaḥ । anyonyapratiṣedho vipratiṣedhaḥ ।

[Meaning] What do you mean by vipratiṣedha? Vipratiṣedha word is formed from root √sidh prefixed with 'vi' and suffixed with '–ghañ'. Mutual opposition between the two is vipratiṣedha. Mutual blocking between two is pratiṣedha.

Accordingly, vipratiṣedha means mutual blocking or mutual opposition.

Great grammarian and Vedic scholar of 19th century India, Maharshi Dayanand Saraswati, while commenting upon this sūtra in his Aṣṭādhyāyī-Bhāṣyam, observes as:

विप्रतिषेध में (विरोध होने पर) पर का कार्य होना चाहिए। इतरेतरप्रतिषेधो विप्रतिषेधः – जो परस्पर एक दूसरे का रोकना है वह विप्रतिषेध कहलाता है।

[Meaning] That in vipratiṣedha (opposition) operation of para takes place. Mutual blocking or mutual opposition is called vipratiṣedha.

Thus as per Mahābhāṣyakāra and modern Pāṇinian scholars like Maharshi Dayanand Saraswati, vipratiṣedha always means mutual blocking or mutual opposition and not the rule conflict as other Western scholars meant it.

By the time of Patañjali, one more meaning of vipratiṣedha became prevalent. It was तुल्यबल विरोध (opposition between equally powerful). Patañjali discusses this meaning in detail. In Mahābhāṣya, a question was raised that in the case of equal power of two rules or persons, none of them can operate because the equally powerful rule or person will block the other. Solving this issue, Patañjali says that the sūtra विप्रतिषेधे परं कार्यम् will open the door for the operation of either one among the two equally powerful rules.

This meaning of तुल्यबल विरोध is given importance in Kāśikā. The author of Kāśikā defines तुल्यबल विरोध as:

तुल्यबलविरोधो विप्रतिषेधः। यत्र द्वौ प्रसङ्गावन्यार्थवेकस्मिन् युगपत् प्राप्नुतः, स तुल्यबलविरोधो विप्रतिषेधः। तस्मिन् विप्रतिषेधे परं कार्यं भवति। उत्सर्गापवादनित्यानित्यान्तरङ्गबहिरङ्गेषु तुल्यबलता न अस्तीति न अयमस्य योगस्य विषयः। बलवतैव तत्र भवितव्यम्। अप्रवृत्तौ, पर्यायेण वा प्रवृत्तौ प्राप्तायां वचनमारभ्यते।

tulyabalavirodho vipratiṣedhaḥ। yatra dvau prasaṅgāvanyārthavekasmin yugapat prāpnutaḥ, sa tulyabalavirodho vipratiṣedhaḥ। tasmin vipratiṣedhe paraṁ kāryaṁ bhavati। utsargāpavādanityānityāntaraṅgabahiraṅgeṣu tulyabalatā na astīti na ayamasya yogasya viṣayaḥ। balavataiva tatra bhavitavyam। apravṛttau, paryāyeṇa vā pravṛttau prāptāyāṁ vachanamārabhyate।

[Meaning] The word विप्रतिषेध means 'opposition of rules of equal force.' When two rules having different objects find their common operand simultaneously, that opposition of equal forces is called vipratiṣedha. In vipratiṣedha, the operation of para will take place. A general rule (utsarga) and its exception (apavāda); an invariable (nitya) and an optional (anitya) rule; and an antaraṅga and a bahiraṅga rule, do not have equal force, so they are not the subject of this rule. For the application of these rules, sūtras had to be equally powerful. The rule that has operated elsewhere independently or operated alternatively is called powerful.

As such, if we interpret vipratiṣedha as tulyabala-virodha, there is no problem with the operation of this sūtra. The tradition has discovered many ways of interpreting the same rule.

Following Mahābhāṣyakāra Patañjali and Maharshi Dayanand Saraswati, the student also interprets 'vipratiṣedha' as mutual opposition (p. 35). Still, he fails to acknowledge any of them; it shows that either he did not do a literature review properly or he himself wants to take credit for such interpretations as has already been done by Pāṇinian and post-Pāṇinian scholars. He reads as under:

> 'Note that even though in the previous chapter I frequently used the phrase 'rule conflict' - which has acquired a very specific connotation in modern Pāṇinian scholarship - to discuss the traditional and modern interpretations of 1.4.2, I have not used this phrase in the context of my own interpretation of 1.4.2. I interpret vipratiṣedha 'mutual opposition' as 'DOI' and not as 'rule conflict .'DOI and rule conflict are different concepts. I will discuss this topic in detail later in this chapter.'

The above reference makes it clear that he is borrowing his interpretation from Mahābhāṣyakāra and Maharshi Dayanand Saraswati but is not willing to acknowledge them. This is an example of academic piracy. To conceal this fact, he is giving more emphasis on the Kāśikā's interpretation of vipratiṣedha as 'tulyabala-virodha' 'conflicts between rules of equal strength (p. 45).

Now we come to the 2nd step of interpretation of vipratiṣedha. The concept of mutual interpretation has been explained further by Mahābhāṣyakāra as well as by Maharshi Dayanand Saraswati. Mahābhāṣyakāra observes:

कः पुनर्विप्रतिषेधः ? द्वौ प्रसङ्गावन्यार्थावेकस्मिन्स विप्रतिषेधः ॥ १ ॥ द्वौ प्रसङ्गौ यदान्यार्थौ भवत एकस्मिंश्च युगपत्प्राप्नुतः स विप्रतिषेधः ।

kaḥ punarvipratiṣedhaḥ ? dvau prasaṅgāvanyārthāvekasminsa vipratiṣedhaḥ // 1 // dvau prasaṅgau yadānyārthau bhavata ēkasmiṁścha yugapatprāpnutaḥ sa vipratiṣedhaḥ /

[Meaning] What is this vipratiṣedha? Vipratiṣedha means the application of two rules simultaneously with different objectives at one and the same place (vārttika). That is when two rules with different motives become simultaneously applicable to one item/place; that is called vipratiṣedha.

Maharshi Dayanand also clarifies the 2nd step of interpretation in his Aṣṭādhyāyī Bhāṣya as under:

द्वौ प्रसङ्गौ यदाऽन्यार्थौ भवतः एकस्मिंश्च युगपत् प्राप्नुतः स विप्रतिषेधः ।

dvau prasaṅgau yadā'nyārthau bhavataḥ ēkasmiṁścha yugapat prāpnutaḥ sa vipratiṣedhaḥ /

[Meaning] When two rules with different objectives simultaneously apply at one and the same place, that is called vipratiṣedha'.

Thus in simple language, vipratiṣedha is simultaneous application of two rules with different motives at one place.

But the student speculates vipratiṣedha to mean mutual opposition between operands and not rules (p. 39), as it suits his DOI concept.

As already discussed above, the opposition between two rules with different motives can be understood, but the opposition between two operands is not understandable. This is a totally absurd idea and interpretation. Can the student explain this opposition between operands? Why should they oppose each other? He is trying to rise above Patañjali, so he should be ready to give justification for his speculations. We must keep in mind, in Sanskrit grammar, nothing can be speculative, and there should be justification for all that we try to conceive. As such, this idea of DOI and mutual opposition between two operands is baseless and anti-Pāṇini.

Asiddha and Asiddhvat in Pāṇini

Let me inform at the outset that the term asiddha in tradition has been used to denote all śāstrāsiddha, kāryāsiddha, and asiddhvat. When we say asiddha, that automatically means śāstrāsiddha, or kāryāsiddha or asiddhvat as per context. To understand this properly, we must know the meaning of siddha. Pāṇini and other Āchāryas used this term to denote the meaning of 'known'. Similarly, asiddha will mean unknown. These terms are synonymous to currently used terms 'prasiddha' (well-known) and 'aprasiddha' (not well-known). When we say that something is 'prasiddha' (well-known) or 'siddha' (known), that means that the thing exits and its existence is also acknowledged by people. Similarly, when we say that something is asiddha, that means that though the thing exists, but is unknown to the people and so not acknowledged. But these days western scholars are taking the term asiddha to mean suspended which does not convey actual intention of Pāṇini or of other Āchāryas. When we mean 'asiddha' as 'suspended', it creates confusion.

In the 5th chapter of his thesis, the student deals with three famous rules of the *Aṣṭādhyāyī* dealing with the concepts of *asiddha* and *asiddhavat.*

6.1.86 षत्वतुकोरसिद्धः *ṣatvatukor asiddhaḥ*

8.2.1 पूर्वत्रासिद्धम् *pūrvatrāsiddham*

6.4.22 असिद्धवदत्राभात् *asiddhavad atrā bhāt*

Now we shall take up for analysis all the above rules one by one.

Ṣatvatukor asiddhaḥ - Pāṇini 6.1.86

The correct interpretation of the sūtra 6.1.86 *ṣatvatukor asiddhaḥ* is as under:

'A single replacement (*ekādeśaḥ*) in place of the preceding and the following sounds in *saṁhitā* (extreme proximity of phonemes or, more aptly, juxtaposition/euphonic combination remains) unknown (so, unacknowledged) for replacement with 'ṣ' or augment 'tuk'.'

While presenting the English translation of the above sūtra in the name of traditional interpretation, the student reads as:

'A single replacement (ekaḥ) in place of the preceding and the following sound segments (pūrvaparayoḥ) in continuous utterance (saṁhitāyām) is suspended (asiddhaḥ) for any potential replacement with ṣ or insertion of augment tUK (ṣatva-tuk-or).'

The student does not mention any source which he has taken this traditional translation from. So, it is understood that this is what he understood from traditionalists' translations.

First, he translates the word saṅhitā as 'continuous utterance' which is incorrect. As per Pāṇini, saṅhitā is extreme proximity of phonemes. परः सन्निकर्षः संहिता-1.4.109. So, 'continuous utterance' is not a proper meaning. 'Continuous utterance' may also take place even when the phonemes are not in extreme proximity or, say, juxtaposed position. Moreover, he translates 'ṣatva' as a potential replacement with 'ṣ,' which can also be read as a replacement with 'ṣ'; potential meaning is inherited in the word replacement itself.

Now we come to the analysis part of the interpretation of the above sūtra done by the student. He writes:

> 'Here, should the kārya (i.e., 'operation', or more aptly, 'outcome of the application of the rule') be suspended or the śāstra (i.e., the rule) itself? In traditional literature, if the kārya is suspended, this is called kāryāsiddhi, whereas if the śāstra is suspended, this is called śāstrāsiddhi. According to the Kāśikā, asiddha implies kāryāsiddhi, but according to the Siddhānta-Kaumudī, asiddha stands for śāstrāsiddhi.'

In the above analysis, the student quotes two different views regarding the interpretation of 'asiddha' in the sūtra. One view of Kāśikā, which takes asiddha for 'kāryāsiddha (unknown operation)', another that of

Bhaṭṭoji Dixit, who takes asiddha for śāstrāsiddha (unknown rule). Here we can easily understand that there is no material difference if we say kāryāsiddha (operation is not known) and the śāstrāsiddha (rule is not known). If kārya is not known, the sūtra (rule) teaching that kārya will also automatically considered to be unknown. Similarly, if the śāstra (rule) is not known, its kārya will automatically be not known. If one is able to understand it, the whole problem is over. I have seen that many scholars use these words but do not know their intended meaning. Our student is also suffering from the same problem. He says that in traditional literature, if the kārya is suspended, this is called kāryāsiddhi, whereas if the śāstra is suspended, this is called śāstrāsiddhi. He explains the concept of śāstrāsiddhi with the help of Nyāsa (8.2.1), which defines śāstrāsiddhi as:

शास्त्रस्यासिद्धौ च कृतायामर्थतः कार्यासिद्धत्वं कृतमेव भवति; तस्य तन्निबन्धनत्वात्।

śāstrasyāsiddhau ca kṛ tāyām arthataḥ kāryāsiddhatvaṁ kṛ tam eva bhavati tasya tannibandhanatvāt.

[Meaning] When śāstra (rule) is made asiddha (unknown), its operation is also automatically made unknown, as the operation is included in the rule.

His explanation is as under:

> 'Rule X is asiddha with respect to rule Y. However, when rule X (śāstra) is asiddha with respect to rule Y, the outcome of the application of rule X (kārya) too will automatically be asiddha with respect to rule Y. In other words, I think that śāstrāsiddhi always entails kāryāsiddhi.'

There is not problem with this explanation, but it appears that he has avoided the meaning of kāryāsiddha (unknown operation) in the context of tradition. Nyāsa (8.2.1) has also explained the meaning of kāryāsiddha (unknown operation) as under:

कार्यासिद्धत्वाश्रयणे हि यथा देवदत्तस्य हन्तरि हते न पुनर्देवदत्तस्य प्रादुर्भावो भवति, तथा कार्यस्यासिद्धत्वे प्रतिपादिते न पुनः प्रकृतेः प्रत्यापत्तिर्भवति ।

kāryāsiddhatvāśrayaṇe hi yathā devadattasya hantari hate na punardevadattasya prādurbhāvo bhavati, tathā kāryasyāsiddhatve pratipādite na punaḥ prakṛteḥ pratyāpattirbhavati ।

[Meaning] Once the kārya (operation) of a sūtra or śāstra is made unknown, then its prakṛti (sūtra) cannot be deemed as operative or restored, just as the life of Devadatta cannot be restored even when his killer gets killed.

In other words, here, kāryāsiddhi means 'unknown operation'. That is, the operation of sūtra will take place, but it will not be acknowledged to have taken place.

Now we can infer from the foregoing explanations that there is no difference between the concept of śāstrāsiddha (unknown or unacknowledged rule) and kāryāsiddha (unknown or unacknowledged operation), because if the rule is unknown or unacknowledged,, its operation also automatically stands unknown or unacknowledged, similarly if the operation is unknown or unacknowledged, its rule also automatically stands unknown or unacknowledged.

Given his misunderstanding of śāstrāsiddha, the student expresses his opinion that in sūtra *ṣatvatukor asiddhaḥ*, the term asiddha (unknown or unacknowledged) stands for śāstrāsiddhi (unknown or unacknowledged rule) only (p. 173).

But the fact is that, contrary to his claim, the term 'asiddha' (unknown or unacknowledged) in the sūtra under discussion stands for both śāstrāsiddha (unknown or unacknowledged rule) and kāryāsiddha unknown or unacknowledged kārya). The student himself quoted two different examples about this sūtra

a). adhī + ktvā – 'to study'

b). kas + asiñcat 'Who sprinkled?

He thinks both of the above examples belong to the śāstrāsiddhi. But the reality is that the first example, 'adhī + ktvā', belongs to kāryāsiddhi (unknown or unacknowledged operation), and the second example, 'kas + asiñcat' belongs to śāstrāsiddhi (unknown or unacknowledged rule). I am going to illustrate it below:

a). *adhī + ktvā* – 'to study'

इण् (गतौ, अदादिः, २.४०)

→ अधि + इ + क्त्वा [by समानकर्तृकयोः पूर्वकाले ३.४.२१, क्त्वा-प्रत्ययः]

→ अधी + त्वा [by अकः सवर्णे दीर्घः ६.१.१०१, short vowel 'I' replaced by long vowel 'ī']

→ अधी + ल्यप् [by समासेऽनञ्पूर्वे क्त्वो ल्यप् ७.१.३७, क्त्वा- प्रत्यय replaced by ल्यप्]

→ अधी + तुक् + य [kāryāsiddhi (unacknowledged or unknown operation of 'ī'), so by sūtra ह्रस्वस्य पिति कृति तुक् ६.१.७१), tuk augment takes place]

→ अधी + त् + य [by ककारस्य हलन्त्यम् १.३.३, इत् sañjñā of 'k' of tuk and by तस्य लोपः १.३.९, the same 'k' is elided, 'u' also elided]

→ अधीत्य [final form]

b). iṇ (gatau, adādigaṇa, 2.40)

→ adhi + i + ktvā [by *samānakartṛkayoḥ pūrvakāle* 3.4.21, ktvā-pratyaya]

→ adhī + tvā [by *akaḥ savarṇe dīrghaḥ* 6.1.101, short vowel 'I' replaced by long vowel 'ī']

→ adhī + lyap [by *samāse'nañpūrve ktvo lyap* 7.1.37, ktvā-pratyaya replaced by lyap]

→ adhī + tuk + ya [by *piti kṛti tuk* 6.1.71, tuk augment permitted due to kāryāsiddha (unknown or unacknowledged operation 'ī' by sūtra- 6.1.101]

→ adhī + t + ya [by *kakārasya halantyam* 1.3.3, *it* sañjñā of final 'k' of tuk and by tasya lopaḥ 1.3.9 'u' also elided]

→ adhītya (final form)

Above is the example of स्थानी लक्षण कार्य or kāryāsiddhi, as the kārya of sūtra 6.1.101 has taken place, but remained unknown or unacknowledged by sūtra 6.1.71, so the same will operate, whereas in normal conditions it would not have operated because of long 'I'.

But our student is totally confused and proving it the example of śāstrāsiddhi. He does not know what does he want to say? He reads:

> 'Thus, we deem both 6.1.101 *akaḥ savarṇe dīrghaḥ* and the outcome of its application (because, remember, śāstrāsiddhi always entails kāryāsiddhi) to be suspended with respect to the rule 6.1.71 *hrasvasya piti kṛti tuk*, which teaches that augment tUK is attached to a verbal base ending in a short

vowel when a kṛt affix marked with P follows. Therefore, we consider adhīya to be adhi-i-ya, apply 6.1.71 to it, and get the correct form adhītya.'

Now we shall take up the example of śāstrāsiddha (unknown or unacknowledged rule).

b). *kas + asiñcat* 'Who sprinkled?

→ कस् + असिंचत् =

→ कर् + असिंचत् (the स changed to र by ससजुषो रुः ८.२.६६)

→ क उ + असिंचत् (उ being substituted for र by अतो रोरप्लुतादप्लुते ६.१.११३)

→ को + असिंचत् (अ + उ = ओ आद्गुणः - ६.१.८७)

→ कोऽसिंचत् (ओ + अ = ओ एङः पदान्तादति -६.१.१०९).

→ कोऽसिंचत् (final form)

→ kas + asiñchat

→ kar + asiñchat [the स changed to र by ससजुषो रुः ८.२.६६']

→ k u + asiñchat [उ being substituted for र by अतो रोरप्लुतादप्लुते ६.१.११३]

→ ko + asiñchat [अ + उ = ओ आद्गुणः - ६.१.८७]

→ ko' asiñchat [ओ + अ = ओ एङः पदान्तादति -६.१.१०९]

→ ko'asiñchat (final form)

By आदेशप्रत्यययोः 8.3.59, स coming after ओ required to be changed into ष, but here the rule teaching single-replacement ओ is considered to be asiddha (unknown) for this purpose by sūtra षत्वतुकोरसिद्धः 6.1.86, so it could not operate. This is the example of आदेश-लक्षण प्रतिषेध (prohibition of replacement rule) or śāstrāsiddhi (unknown rule).

Here it may also be informed that Patañjali also supports both śāstrāsiddhi (unknown rule) and kāryāsiddhi (unknown operation) in the examples of ko'siñchat and adhītya, respectively, in his commentary on the sūtra, under discussion. He observes as follows.

षत्वतुकोरसिद्धः ।। 6.1.86

Ṣatvatukorasiddhaḥ (6.1.86)

किमर्थमिदमुच्यते?

kimarthamidamuchyate?

Why it is taught?

षत्वतुकोरसिद्धवचनमादेशलक्षणप्रतिषेधार्थमुत्सर्गलक्षणभावार्थं च ।। 1

ṣatvatukorasiddhavachanamādeśalakṣaṇapratiṣedhārtha mutsargalakṣaṇabhāvārthaṁ cha. 1

Ṣatvatukorasiddhaḥ (6.1.86) is taught for the prohibition of replacement rule and operation of general rule.

षत्वतुकोरसिद्धत्वमुच्यते, आदेशलक्षणप्रतिषेधार्थमुत्सर्गलक्षणभावार्थं च ।

ṣatvatukorasiddhatvamuchyate, ādeśalakṣaṇapratiṣ-edhārthamutsargalakṣaṇabhāvārthaṁ cha.

That is, *ṣatvatukorasiddhaḥ* is taught, so that replacement rule is prohibited and general rule is operated (due to unknown operation of replacement).

आदेशलक्षणप्रतिषेधार्थं तावत् - कोऽसिञ्चत्, सोऽसिञ्चत् । एकादेशे कृते इण इति षत्वं प्राप्नोति। असिद्धत्वान्न भवति । उत्सर्गलक्षणभावार्थं च - अधीत्य, प्रेत्य। एकादेशे कृते ह्रस्वस्य - इति तुग्न प्राप्नोति, असिद्धत्वाद्भवति ॥ अस्ति प्रयोजनमेतत्। किं तर्हीति?

ādeśalakṣaṇapratiṣedhārthaṁ tāvat - ko'siñchat,

so'siñchat । ēkādeśe kṛte iṇa iti ṣatvaṁ prāpnoti । asiddhatvānna bhavati । utsargalakṣaṇabhāvārthaṁ cha - adhītya, pretya । ēkādeśe kṛte hrasvasya - iti tugna prāpnoti, asiddhatvādbhavati ॥ asti prayojanametat । kiṁ tarhīti?

The examples of the prohibition of replacement sūtra are कोऽसिञ्चत्, सोऽसिञ्चत्. By sūtra आदेशप्रत्यययोः 8.3.59 स coming after ओ requires to be changed into ष, but here the rule teaching single-replacement ओ is considered to be prohibited for this purpose, so could not operate. Examples of operation of general rule are – adhītya and pretya. When sūtra 7.1.37 replaces ktvā-pratyaya with 'lyap', sūtra *piti kṛti tuk* 6.1.71 teaching insertion of 'tuk' augment after short 'i' of adhi becomes operational. But the same cannot operate as the short 'i' of adhi has been made long already by *akaḥ savarṇe dīrghaḥ* 6.1.101. Here, due to *kāryāsiddhi* (unknown operation or kārya), the operation of the same takes place. Is this the purpose of the sūtra? Yes.

तत्रोत्सर्गलक्षणाप्रसिद्धिरुत्सर्गाभावात् ।। 2

tatrotsargalakṣaṇāprasiddhirutsargābhāvāt ।। 2

Here the general rule operation (kārya) is unknown (invisible), because the general rule is also unknown (invisible).

तत्रोत्सर्गलक्षणस्य कार्यस्याप्रसिद्धिः। अधीत्य, प्रेत्य । किं कारणम् ? उत्सर्गाभावात् । ह्रस्वस्येति । उच्यते, न चात्र ह्रस्वं पश्यामः ॥ ननु चात्राप्यसिद्धवचनात्सिद्धम् ॥

tatrotsargalakṣaṇasya kāryasyāprasiddhiḥ । adhītya, pretya । kiṁ kāraṇam ? utsargābhāvāt । hrasvasyeti । uchyate, na chātra hrasvaṁ paśyamaḥ ॥ nanu chātrāpyasiddhavachanātsiddham ॥

Here the operation of the general rule is unknown in the examples of adhītya and pretya. Why? Since the general rule teaching long 'ī' is also unknown. Otherwise sūtra *piti kṛti tuk* 6.1.71 that teaches insertion of 'tuk' augment after the short 'i' of adhi will not operate. Since it sees the short vowel, so operates. This process also took place due to unknown operation of general rule. There is a vārttika:

असिद्धवचनात्सिद्धमिति चेन्नान्यस्यासिद्धवचनादन्यस्य भावः । 3

asiddhavachanātsiddhamiti chennānyasyāsiddhavachanādanyasya bhāvaḥ । 3

Do you want to say that if unknown operation of a sūtra makes the sūtra known. It is not like that. If operation is declared unknown, sūtra cannot become known.

असिद्धवचनात्सिद्धमिति चेत्, तन्न । किं कारणम् ? नान्यस्यासिद्धवचनादन्यस्य भावः । न ह्यन्यस्यासिद्धवचनादन्यस्य प्रादुर्भावो भवति । न हि देवदत्तस्य हन्तरि हते देवदत्तस्य प्रादुर्भावो भवति ॥

asiddhavachanātsiddhamiti chet, tanna । kiṁ kāraṇam? nānyasyāsiddhavachanādanyasya bhāvaḥ । na hyanyasyāsiddhavachanādanyasya prādurbhāvo bhavati । na hi devadattasya hantari hate devadattasya prādurbhāvo bhavati ॥

Do you want to say that unknown operation of a sūtra makes the sūtra known. It is not like that. Why? If one (sūtra or its kārya) is unknown, another (kārya or sūtra) cannot be considered known.

Unknown operation of a sūtra cannot make the sūtra known or restored, just as the life of Devadatta cannot be restored even when his killer gets killed. So, the Vārttikakāra says :

तस्मात्स्थानिवद्वचनमसिद्धत्वं च (4)

tasmātsthānivadvachanamasiddhatvaṁ cha | 4

तस्मात्स्थानिवद्भावो वक्तव्यः, असिद्धत्वं च । अधीत्ये, प्रेत्येति स्थानिवद्भावः । कोऽसिञ्चत्, सोऽसिञ्चदित्यत्रासिद्धत्वम् ॥

tasmātsthānivadbhāvo vaktavyaḥ, asiddhatvaṁ cha | adhītye, pretyeti sthānivadbhāvaḥ | ko'siñchat, so'siñchadityatrāsiddhatvam ||

Thus asiddha represents both operation and prohibition of replacement rule. In adhītya and pretya, replacement with long vowel is unknown, so sūtra teaching tuk augment operates and in ko'siñchat, so'asiñchat, sūtra teaching replacement of स after ओ with ष prohibited.

स्थानिवद्वचनानर्थक्यं शास्त्रासिद्धत्वात् । 5

sthānivadvachanānarthakyaṁ śāstrāsiddhatvāt | 5

स्थानिवद्वचनमनर्थकम् । किं कारणम्? शास्त्रासिद्धत्वात् । नानेन कार्यस्यासिद्धत्वं क्रियते । किं तर्हि ? शास्त्रासिद्धत्वमनेन क्रियते । एकादेशशास्त्रं तुक्शास्त्रेऽसिद्धं भवतीति ॥

sthānivadvachanamanarthakam | kiṁ kāraṇam ? śāstrāsiddhatvāt | nānena kāryasyāsiddhatvaṁ kriyate | kiṁ tarhi ? śāstrāsiddhatvamanena kriyate | ēkādeśaśāstraṁ tukśāstre'siddhaṁ bhavatīti ||

If you say that kārya or operation of replacement (kāryāsiddhi) is meaningless, because the same can be done by śāstrāsiddhi (making rule asiddha or unknown). Here it is said that śāstrāsiddhi cannot be helpful in kāryāsiddhi. Why? If we make the rule asiddha, then the rule teaching ekādeśa (single replacement) of lengthening of 'ī' will become asiddha (unknown) with respect to the rule teaching 'tuk' augment in the word adhītya, and thus we shall get the final form adhitya and not adhītya.

Now, it should be clear why Kāśikākāra and Bhaṭṭoji Dixit have used different terms - kāryāsiddha and śāstrāsiddha- to denote 'asiddha' in the sūtra, because they denote the same purpose. It never means that they were not aware of the two meanings of asiddha- as kāryāsiddha and śāstrāsiddha. Kāśikā has not quoted any example where ṣatva replacement is required. It quoted कोऽस्य, योऽस्य, कोऽस्मै, योऽस्मै. All these examples do not require ṣatva. But it talks about ṣatva as a matter of principle. He dealt with the example of adhītya practically, where tuk augment is required. In the example of adhītya, there is the occasion of kāryāsiddhi, so he called it 'kāryāsiddhi'. He says:

षत्वे तुकि च कर्तव्ये एकदेशोऽसिद्धो भवति, सिद्धकार्यं न करोति इत्यर्थः। असिद्धवचनमादेशलक्षणप्रतिषेधर्थम्, उत्सर्गलक्षणभावार्थं च। कोऽसिचदित्यत्र एङः पदान्तादति ६.१.१०९ इति एकादेशस्य परं प्रत्यादिवद्भावातपदादेरिण उत्तरस्य आदेशस्य सकारस्य षत्वं प्राप्नोति, तदसिद्धत्वान् न भवति। कोऽस्य, योऽस्य, कोऽस्मै, योऽस्मै इत्येकादेशस्य असिद्धत्वातिणः इति षत्वं न भवति। तुग्विधौ अधीत्य, प्रेत्य इत्यत्र एकादेशस्य असिद्धत्वात् ह्रस्वस्य पिति कृति तुक् ६.१.७१ इति तुग् भवति।

ṣatve tuki cha kartavye ēkadeśo'siddho bhavati, siddhakāryaṁ na karoti ityarthaḥ । asiddhavachanamādeśalakṣaṇapratiṣedhartham, utsargalakṣaṇabhāvārthaṁ cha । ko'sichadityatra ēṅaḥ padāntādati 6.1.109 iti ēkādeśasya paraṁ pratyādivadbhāvātapadāderiṇa uttarasya ādeśasya sakārasya ṣatvaṁ prāpnoti, tadasiddhatvān na bhavati । ko'sya, yo'sya, ko'smai, yo'smai ityekādeśasya asiddhatvātiṇaḥ iti । ṣatvaṁ na bhavati tugvidhau adhītya, pretya ityatra ēkādeśasya asiddhatvāt hrasvasya piti kṛti tuk 6.1.71 iti tug bhavati ।

Similarly, Bhaṭṭoji Dixit's main emphasis was on the example of ko'sichat requiring śāstrāsiddhi, so he mentioned the word śāstrāsiddhi. He did not give any emphasis about the examples which required kāryāsiddhi. He quoted two examples adhītya and pretya, wherein adhītya required kāryāsiddhi and pretya did not require kāryāsiddhi. I quote him as under:

षत्वे तुकि च कर्तव्ये एकादेशशास्त्रमसिद्धं स्यात् । कोऽसिचत् । इह षत्वं न । अधीत्य । प्रेत्य । ह्रस्वस्य- (कौमुदी-२८५८) इति तुक् ॥

ṣatve tuki cha kartavye ēkādeśaśāstramasiddhaṁ syāt । *ko'sichat* । *iha ṣatvaṁ na* । *adhītya* । *pretya* । *hrasvasya- (kaumudī-2858) iti tuk* ॥

Is Sūtra ससजुषो रुः (8.2.66-) asiddh with respect to अतो रोरप्लुतादप्लुते (6.1.113)?

Regarding the application of sūtras ससजुषो रुः (8.2.66-) and अतो रोरप्लुतादप्लुते (6.1.113) cited above, the student also faces a problem, so he thinks it is worthy of discussion. According to him, '8.2.66 *sasajuṣoḥ ruḥ* is asiddha with respect to 6.1.113 *ato ror aplutād aplute* by 8.2.1 *pūrvatrāsiddham*. Therefore, 6.1.113 cannot acknowledge 8.2.66 and the outcome of its application cannot apply there. But this contradicts with what we observe in the derivation of ko'siñcat. To get the correct final form, we ought to apply 6.1.113 to kar + asiñcat, which is the direct outcome of the application of 8.2.66.

He further observes that Nyāsa on 6.1.113 also acknowledges this problem but is unable to solve it. According to him, 'Nyāsa says that the only 'ru' that we find in the Aṣṭādhyāyī results from the application of

8.2.66. So, Pāṇini would not have composed 6.1.113, which applies to 'ru' if he intended for the outcome of the application of 8.2.66 (i.e., ru) to be asiddha with respect to 6.1.113. He also quotes Buiskool (1939: 101), who thinks that Pāṇini has placed 6.1.113 in 6.1 only because of its similarity with the rules that precede and follow it'.

After that, he suggests a possible solution to this problem. He says, 'I think that, in the Pāṇinian system, all possible rules that can be applied while constructing a word ought to be applied before the word enters a sentence. Let us call them word-level rules. Let us call those rules which apply after the word enters the sentence sentence-level rules. I think Pāṇini does not consider word-level rules to be asiddha with respect to sentence-level rules. 8.2.66 is a word-level rule simply because it can be applied before the word enters the sentence, and thus is not asiddha with respect to 6.1.113, which by virtue of applying at the boundary between two words is a sentence-level rule'.

On the basis of the foregoing discussion, one can easily conclude that the student is utterly confused. The solution he suggests creates far greater confusion. He thinks that in Pāṇinian tradition, only Nyāsa could acknowledge it; other grammarians were oblivious to it. That is wrong. Further, whatever he says about Nyāsa also, it is clearly discernible that he could not understand Nyāsa too.

First of all, let me explain in easily understandable terms why para sūtra 8.2.66 *sasajuṣoḥ ruḥ* is siddha (known) to 6.1.113 *ato ror aplutād aplute*, according to tradition, even when its asiddhtva (unknown status) is described by 8.2.1 *pūrvatrāsiddham*?

First of all, let me remind here that the Sanskrit language is a natural language, and the seers have formed its rules and regulations following the laws of nature. Neither is there any artificiality in this language nor can it be understood by an artificial system.

Ato ror aplutād aplute-6.1.113 is the only sūtra that teaches 'utva' of 'ru' taught by 8.2.66 *sasajuṣoḥ ruḥ* in the entire Aṣṭādhyāyī. If the operation of *sasajuṣoḥ ruḥ* is made unknown to *ato ror aplutād aplute*-6.1.113 as per instructions of 8.2.1 *pūrvatrāsiddham*. This sūtra (8.2.66) will not be able to make 'ru' and if it fails to make 'ru', 'utva' of 'ru' cannot be made by *ato ror aplutād aplute*-6.1.113. Under this condition, the sūtra *ato ror aplutād aplute* can never operate because it always needs 'ru' by 8.2.66 for its operation or we can say that it is completely dependent upon 8.2.66 for its operation. If it is not allowed to operate by 8.2.1 *pūrvatrāsiddham*, the sūtra *ato ror aplutād aplute* 6.1.113 will become redundant. This is not only a single case; there are hoards of other cases which will meet the same fate. This condition in grammar is called 'āśraya' or 'base', which means the sūtra *ato ror aplutād aplute* cannot survive without 8.2.66 *sasajuṣoḥ ruḥ*. So, here it requires exemption from the jurisdiction of rule 8.2.1, just as an ambulance carrying a sick person is exempted from all traffic rules and regulations, similarly, the rule that act as āśraya or base for the other rule for its operation is exempted from any rules or regulations blocking its operation. Therefore, although 8.2.66 *sasajuṣoḥ ruḥ* is asiddha (unknown) to 6.1.113 *ato ror aplutād aplute*, according to 8.2.1 *pūrvatrāsiddham*, yet it will be considered as siddha (known), being the āśraya of 6.1.113.

Rule of āśrayasiddhi is also discussed in Mahābhāṣya (6.1.86), while dealing with the issue of siddhatva (acknowledgement) or asiddhatva (unacknowledgement) of pluta (protracted sounds). I quote the exact reference hereunder:

एवं मन्यते - असिद्धः प्लुत आश्रयात्सिद्धो भवति ॥ अथवा यस्यां नाप्राप्तायां परिभाषायामुत्वमारभ्यते, साऽऽश्रयात्सिद्धा स्यात् ।

ēvaṁ manyate - asiddhaḥ pluta āśrayātsiddho bhavati ॥ *athavā yasyāṁ nāprāptāyāṁ paribhāṣāyāmutvamārabhyate, sā''śrayātsiddhā syāt* ।

In Kāśkā (6.1.86), 8.2.66 *sasajuṣoḥ ruḥ* is made known due to its being āśraya of *ato ror aplutād aplute*-6.1.113. I quote the reference below:

रुत्वमपि आश्रयात् पूर्वत्र असिद्धम् ८.२.१ इति असिद्धं न भवति ।

rutvamapi āśrayāt pūrvatra asiddham 8.2.1 iti asiddhaṁ na bhavati ।

Similarly, Nyāsa also acknowledges that 'rutva' from rule 8.2.66 *sasajuṣoḥ ruḥ* is siddha with respect to *ato ror aplutād aplute*-6.1.113, being the āśrya of it (6.1.113). I quote the exact statement below:

ननु चोत्त्वे कर्तव्ये पूर्वत्रासिद्धम् ८.२.१ इति रुत्त्वमसिद्धम्, तदसतो रोः कथमुत्त्वं शक्यते विधातुम्? इत्यत आह -`रुत्वमप्याश्रयात्? सिद्धम्` इति। यदि रुत्वमसिद्धं स्यात्, तदा स्थानित्वेन रोराश्रयणमनर्थकं स्यात्; कस्यचिदुकारानुबन्धविशिष्टस्य रोरसम्भवात् ।

nanu chottve kartavye pūrvatrāsiddham 8.2.1 iti ruttvamasiddham, tadasato roḥ kathamuttvaṁ śakyate vidhātum? ityata āha -`rutvamapyāśrayāt? siddham` iti । *yadi rutvamasiddhaṁ syāt, tadā sthānitvena rorāśrayaṇamanarthakaṁ syāt;*

kasyachidukārānubandhaviśiṣṭasya rorasambhavāt ।

[Meaning] When we make 'u' of 'ru', the sūtra 8.2.66 *sasajuṣoḥ ruḥ* teaching 'ru' is made unknown by *pūrvatrāsiddham* 8.2.1. That being so, how can 'ru' be changed into 'u'. So it is said- the 'rutva' is the base of sūtra (6.1.113) teaching 'utva' of 'rutva'. As such the sūtra (8.2.66) teaching 'rutva' is not considered as unknown. If 'rutva' becomes asiddha (unknown), then 'ru' as the āśraya of its substitute 'u' will become useless. In this condition, no 'ru' will ever be able to change into 'u'.

From the foregoing, one can find out the traditional solution to the above problem. But the student has miserably failed to know the secret of the solution suggested by tradition and seems to be hijacked by his own imaginary hypothesis built upon the wrong interpretation of Kāśikā-vṛtti as pointed out already. I again quote his interpretation of Nyāsa

> 'Nyāsa says that the only ru that we find in the Aṣṭādhyāyī results from the application of 8.2.66. So Pāṇini would not have composed 6.1.113 which applies to ru if he intended for the outcome of the application of 8.2.66 (i.e., ru) to be asiddha with respect to 6.1.113.'

One can easily find the difference among what the Patañjali, Kāśikā and Nyāsa intend to say, and how the intended sense of Nyāsa has been distorted by the student due to ignorance.

Pūrvatrāsiddham- Pāṇini 8.2.1

The meaning of the above sūtra given by the student is rendered hereunder:

'That which is taught from here onwards is suspended (asiddham) with respect to what precedes it (pūrvatra).'

He rewrites this traditional interpretation in the form of a syllogism as follows

'As per the tradition's interpretation, 8.2.1 can be rewritten as follows: Q is suspended with respect to P if:

Q is taught after P in the serial order of the Aṣṭādhyāyī, and

Q is taught after 8.2.1 in the serial order of the Aṣṭādhyāyī.'

The above syllogism is correct. But had he used the term unknown for suspended, it would been more clear. In this matter, his question regarding 'Kāśikā using the term kāryāsiddha and Bhaṭṭoji Dixit using śāstrāsiddha' for asiddha has already been answered.

Asiddhavad atrā bhāt- Pāṇini 6.4.22

Let me first give the translation of the above rule, as is intended by Kātyāyana, Patañjali and Kāśikā

'Sūtra starting here up to the jurisdiction of 'bha' (i.e. end of the pāda or 6.4.175) operates as asiddhvat or as if unknown to another sūtra if both sūtras have (samānāśraya) a common āśraya (base/cause/place) of action.

Note: Here āśraya means base, place or cause of action.

Now I quote the traditional meaning of the above sūtra as understood by the student.

'That which is taught in the section starting here and extending up to bha (ā bhāt) is suspended (asiddhavat), if both rules have a samānāśraya 'common substratum' (atra)'.

The traditional translation of the above sūtra known to the student shows that he is in utter confusion. He could not understand the real meaning of the sūtra as intended by Pāṇini and other grammarians of his tradition.

He could not understand the interpretation of all three parts of the sūtra- 'ā bhāt', 'assidhvat' and 'atra' and declares in open defiance as (p. 181) 'I disagree with Kāśikā's interpretation of all three parts of this rule, namely 'asiddhavat', 'ā bhāt' and 'atra'.

Now we shall take into consideration all three parts one by one.

So far as 'ā bhāt' is concerned, the student translates 'bh' as up to 'bha'. He is not able to understand the meaning of 'bha' here. He complaints that both the Kāśikā and the Siddhānta-Kaumudī interpret 'ā bhāt', not as 'up to 6.4.129 bhasya', but instead as 'up to the end of the section headed by 6.4.129 bhasya'. The jurisdiction of 6.4.129 continues up to 6.4.175, which is the end of 6.4. Thus, according to the Kāśikā, 'ā bhāt' implies 'up to the end of 6.4'. He also quotes Kāśikā (6.4.22).

यदित ऊर्ध्वमनुक्रमिष्यामः आ अध्यायपरिसमाप्तेः तदसिद्धवत् भवति इत्येवं वेदितव्यम्। आ भातिति विषयनिर्देशः।

yad ita ūrdhvam anukramiṣyāmaḥ ā adhyāyaparisamāpteḥ tad asiddhavat bhavati ity evaṁ veditavyam. ā bhātiti viṣayanirdeśaḥ ।

[Meaning] Now rules starting from here and extending up to the end of the chapter operate like asiddhvat or as if unknown, this may be known to us. Here the word 'ā bhāt' means up to the 'viṣaya' or jurisdiction of 'bha'.

But the student is not able to understand the meaning of आ भातीति विषयनिर्देशः।

He finds Kātyāyana and Patañjali discussing both possibilities:

> 'One, that the jurisdiction of 6.4.22 ends at 6.4.129, and the other, that it continues up to the end of 6.4. We will study this later in this chapter.'

Let me clarify here that the student is confused and not able to understand Patañjali's Mahābhāṣya. It is not so easy to understand his commentary. Patañjali has discussed the issue of whether 'ābhāt' in the sūtra excludes the jurisdiction of *bhasya* 6.4.129 or includes the jurisdiction of *bhasya* 6.4.129. I furnish the whole discussion below:

किं पुनः प्राग्भादसिद्धम्, आहोस्वित्सह तेन ? कुतः पुनरयं सन्देहः ? आङाऽयं निर्देशः क्रियते, आङ् च पुनः सन्देहं जनयति । तद्यथा - आ पाटलिपुत्रात् वृष्टो देव इति सन्देहः - किं प्राक् पाटलिपुत्रात् - सह तेनेति । एवमिहापि सन्देहः - प्राग्भात् - सह तेनेति । कश्चात्र विशेषः?

प्राग्भादिति चेच्छुनामघोनाभूगुणेषूपसंख्यानम्।

प्राग्भादिति चेच्छुनामघोनाभूगुणेषूपसंख्यानं कर्तव्यम् । शुनः पश्य, शुना, शुने। संप्रसारणे कृते अल्लोपोऽनः ६.४.१३४ इति प्राप्नोति । यस्य पुनः सह तेनासिद्धत्वम्, असिद्धत्वात्तस्य न संयोगाद्वमन्तात् इति प्रतिषेधो भविष्यति॥ यस्यापि प्राग्भादसिद्धत्वं तस्याप्येष न दोषः । कथम् ? नास्त्यत्र विशेषः - अल्लोपेन निवृत्तौ सत्याम्, पूर्वत्वेन वा निवृत्तौ ॥

kiṁ punaḥ prāgbhādasiddham, āhosvitsaha tena ?

kutaḥ punarayaṁ sandehaḥ ? āṅā'yaṁ nirdeśaḥ kriyate, āṅ cha punaḥ sandehaṁ janayati । tadyathā - ā pāṭaliputrāt vṛṣṭo deva iti sandehaḥ - kiṁ prāk pāṭaliputrāt - saha teneti । ēvamihāpi sandehaḥ - prāgbhāt - saha teneti । kaśchātra viśeṣaḥ?

prāgbhāditi chechchhunāmaghonābhūguṇeṣūpasaṁkhyānam ।

prāgbhāditi chechchhunāmaghonābhūguṇeṣūpasaṁkhyānaṁ kartavyam । śunaḥ paśya, śunā, śune । saṁprasāraṇe kṛte allopo'naḥ 6.4.134 iti prāpnoti । yasya punaḥ saha tenāsiddhatvam, asiddhatvāttasya na saṁyogādvamantāt iti pratiṣedho bhaviṣyati ॥ yasyāpi prāgbhādasiddhatvaṁ tasyāpyeṣa na doṣaḥ । katham ? nāstyatra viśeṣaḥ - allopena nivṛttau satyām, pūrvatvena vā nivṛttau ॥

Thus from the foregoing discussion, it is proved that Kātyāyana and Patañjali are not discussing both possibilities: one, that the jurisdiction of 6.4.22 ends at 6.4.129, and the other, that it continues up to the end of 6.4 as suggested by the student. Rather in the above reference, they discuss whether the adhikāra of sūtra 6.4.22 ends before the jurisdiction of 'bha' or at the jurisdiction of 'bha'.

Now we shall discuss the second term 'atra'. Patañjali quoting vārttika from Kātyāyana observes thus:

अत्रग्रहणं विषयार्थम् (2) - विषयः प्रतिनिर्दिश्यते । अत्र - एतस्मिन्नाभाच्छास्त्रे आभाच्छास्त्रमसिद्धं यथा स्यात् । इह मा भूत् - अभाजि, रागः, उपबर्हणमिति ॥

atragrahaṇaṁ viṣayārtham(2)- viṣayaḥ pratinirdiśyate । atra - ētasminnābhāchchhāstre ābhāchchhāstramasiddhaṁ yathā syāt । iha mā bhūt - abhāji, rāgaḥ, upabarhaṇamiti .

[Meaning] Āchārya Pāṇini has chosen the word 'atra' which is intended for giving instructions about the special subject of common āśraya of operation. Here Interpreting the word 'viṣaya' of the Mahābhāṣya, Pradīpa says, '*viśiṣṭo yo viṣayaḥ samānalakṣaṇas tannideśārtham*'. That is, viṣaya means instructions about a special issue of common āśraya of operation/action.

In this section of the jurisdiction of 'bh', one rule operates as if unknown to another having the same āśraya or base/place/cause of operation. Examples are अभाजि and रागः from भञ्ज् and रञ्ज्.

Here the nasals of √ranj and √bhanj have been elided by 6.4.27 घञि च भावकरणयोः — 6.4.28 and 6.4.33 स्यदो जवे before the affixes घञ् and चिण् respectively, and we have the stems रज्, and भज् to which rule 7.2.116 अत उपधायाः applies and we apply vṛddhi of अ preceding the final consonant as भाज् and राज्. Here both rules 6.4.27 and 7.2.116 have a common āśraya/ base of operation, i.e. roots √raj and √bhaj and suffix –ghañ. Had the rule 6.4.27 teaching elision of the nasal been taken as asiddh or unknown to 7.2.116, then अ could not have undergone vṛddhi, as it would not then be उपधा or penultimate. So, here the operation of 6.4.27 was taken as asiddhvat or as if unknown by the present sūtra.

Thus from the above discussion of Mahābhāṣya, it proves that 'atra' stands for common āśraya of operation and the examples quoted in Mahābhāṣya also belong to the common āśraya of operation of both the sūtras 6.427 and 7.2.116. These examples also prove that the word asiddh (unknown) is also used in the sense of asiddhvat (as if unknown).

Moreover, Mahābhāṣyakāra devotes one full para on

the issue of common āśraya of operation in connection with 'atra' as under:

समानाश्रयवचनात्सिद्धम् । समानाश्रयमसिद्धं भवति, व्याश्रयं चैतत् । इह तावत् - पपुषः पश्य, तस्थुषः पश्य, निन्युषः पश्य, चिच्युषः पश्य, युयुवुषः पश्य, लुलुवुषः पश्य - इति - वसावाकारलोपादीनि, वस्वन्तस्य विभक्तौ संप्रसारणम् । पशुष इति - विटि आत्वं, विडन्तस्य विभक्तावाकारलोपः । चाखायिता - चाखायितुमिति - यङ्यात्वम्, यङन्तस्य चार्धधातुके लोप इति ॥ किं वक्तव्यमेतत् ? न हि । कथमनुच्यमानं गंस्यते ?

अत्र ग्रहणसामर्थ्यात् । ननु चान्यदत्रग्रहणस्य प्रयोजनमुक्तम् । किमुक्तम् ? अत्र ग्रहणं विषयार्थमिति । अधिकारादप्येतत्सिद्धम् - इति ॥

samānāśrayavachanātsiddham / samānāśrayamasiddhaṁ bhavati, vyāśrayaṁ chaitat / iha tāvat - papuṣaḥ paśya, tasthuṣaḥ paśya, ninyuṣaḥ paśya, chichyuṣaḥ paśya, yuyuvuṣaḥ paśya, luluvuṣaḥ paśya - iti - vasāvākāralopādīni, vasvantasya vibhaktau saṁprasāraṇam / paśuṣa iti - viṭi ātvaṁ, viḍantasya vibhaktāvākāralopaḥ / chākhāyitā - chākhāyitumiti - yaṅyātvam, yaṅantasya chārdhadhātuke lopa iti // kiṁ vaktavyametat ? na hi / kathamanuchyamānaṁ gaṁsyate ?

atra grahaṇasārmathyāt । nanu chānyadatragrahaṇasya prayojanamuktam । kimuktam ? atra grahaṇaṁ viṣayārthamiti । adhikārādapyetatsiddham - iti ॥

But the student's view about the interpretation of the term 'atra' in Mahābhāṣya is as under:

> 'Now let us examine the word 'atra' in 6.4.22. As stated in section 5.1 of this chapter, Kātyāyana discusses two possible interpretations of the word atra. One is samānāśrayatva 'common substratum' and the other is 'with respect to the rules taught here'. Only one of the two interpretations can be correct, and I think that it is the latter for reasons

that I will now explain. (p.182).'

He further goes on to explain:

'Firstly, notice that in 8.2.1, we find another term which, like a-tra, ends in the affix traL, namely pūrva-tra. There, pūrva-tra means 'with respect to the rules taught before (in the Aṣṭādhyāyī's serial order).' This strongly suggests that in 6.4.22, atra, which also ends in tra, means 'with respect to the rules taught here (in the section governed by 6.4.22)'.'

From the above discussion, it is proved that Kātyāyana and Patañjali do not make two different interpretations of 'atra', rather they make only one interpretation, i.e., common āśraya of operation.

His so-called explanation says that avyaya (indeclinable) 'a-tra' is formed with the suffix a+tral, like pūrvatra is formed from pūrva+tral. But he is not able to understand that 'atra' is an 'avyaya' wherein 'a' does not have an independent existence. On the other hand, in 'pūrvatra', 'pūrva' is a pronoun accepting the ending –tral. So he cannot equate constructions of both. Atra is not formed of a+tral. Moreover, his second part of the explanation is also wrong as it cannot be verified on the ground. He says:

'This strongly suggests that in 6.4.22, atra, which also ends in tra, means 'with respect to the rules taught here (in the section governed by 6.4.22).'

But in the examples of अभाजि and रागः from भञ्ज् and रञ्ज् cited above, we have seen that the rules 6.4.27 घञि च भावकरणयोः 7.2.116 and अत उपधायाः having a common āśraya of operation are not from the same section governed by

6.4.27. The sūtra teaches that the operation of sūtra from this section will remain as asiddhvat (like unknown) to another (which may be from inside or outside this section) having the same base of operation. As such student's second part of the interpretation also does not hold grounds.

Regarding the student's following comments on Kāśikā 6.4.22 and Nyāsa:

> 'According to the Kāśikā on 6.4.22, we must infer samānāśrayatva from the presence of the word atra.
>
> 'The Nyāsa glosses āśraya as nimitta 'cause'. If this is the case, samānāśraya would mean 'common cause'. However, I do not think this is the correct interpretation. I will explain my understanding of the meaning of samānāśraya later in this chapter when discussing a germane example'.

I would say that the student is neither able to interpret samānāśraya correctly as 'cause' following the word 'nimitta' used in Nyāśa, nor his own interpretation is correct. As already discussed above, āśraya according to tradition means base, or instrument or efficient cause, the presence of which is essential for the operation of sūtra. In other words, we may call it a common place or common cause of action. The student tries to translate these technical terms of grammar literally.

Let me inform here that technical terms of any subject cannot be understood by their synonyms. They need to be defined for their proper understanding. Student's problem is that he wants to understand the meaning of technical terms of Pāṇini Vyākaraṇa by their synonyms. So, he is failing everywhere. He needs a good

Guru for his doubts to be addressed.

Now we shall discuss the interpretation of the third part 'asiddhvat' here.

On the basis of the statements of Kāśikā and Siddhāntakaumudi on 6.4.22, he tries to rewrite the traditional interpretation of the rule under discussion as follows:

'i. A is suspended with respect to B if:

ii. both A and B are taught in 6.4.22 – 6.4.175, and

iii. both A and B have a *samānāśraya*

iv. Note that the tradition does not make any actual distinction between *asiddha* and *asiddhavat*, which is why I have translated both terms as 'suspended'.'

Let me observe that the student's understanding of the traditional interpretation of rule 6.4.22 is wrong so far as his ii[nd] interpretation is concerned.

It is not necessary that both A and B are taught in 6.4.22-6.4.175, one of them whose operation will be asiddhvat, had to be from 6.4.22-6.4.175. Another rule may be from outside also. We have also seen in the examples of अभाजि and रागः from भञ्ज् and रञ्ज् cited above, that both the rules 6.4.27 घञि च भावकरणयोः and 7.2.116 अत उपधायाः having a common āśraya of operation are not necessarily to be from 6.4.22-6.4.175. But the rule whose operation will be asiddhvat had to be from the above section, like 6.4.27 घञि च भावकरणयोः in case of अभाजि and रागः.

Let me quote the concerned statement from Kāśikā. It reads as under:

यदित ऊर्ध्वमनुक्रमिष्यामः आ अध्यायपरिसमाप्तेः तदसिद्धवत् भवति इत्येवं वेदितव्यम्।

yad ita ūrdhvam anukramiṣyāmaḥ ā adhyāyaparisamāpteḥ tad asiddhavat bhavati ity evaṁ veditavyam.

[Meaning] It may be known to us that rules starting from here and extending up to the end of the chapter operate like asiddhvat or as if unknown with respect to another having common āśraya of operation.

The above statement of Kāśikā does not approve of students understanding that both A and B are taught in 6.4.22 – 6.4.175. But it says that the rule whose operation will be asiddhvat will be taught in 6.4.22-6.4.175.

Student's iv[th] interpretation

> 'Note that the tradition does not make any actual distinction between asiddha and asiddhavat, which is why I have translated both terms as 'suspended'.'

is also a farfetched one. The tradition knows the distinction between asiddha and asiddhvat. That is why, Kāśikā uses the word तदसिद्धवत् भवति. They also call the word asiddhvat as asiddha.

In the Mahābhāṣya while dealing with the objection on the issue of 'asiddhtva', the term used in the sūtra, it is said that asiddhavat is meant for आदेशलक्षणप्रतिषेधार्थ, i.e. 'prohibition of replacement rule and उत्सर्गलक्षणभावार्थ, operation of general rule (despite its operation is hindered). To verify both objective आदेशलक्षणप्रतिषेधार्थ and उत्सर्गलक्षणभावार्थ, separate examples have been cited in the Mahābhāṣya. For आदेशलक्षणप्रतिषेधार्थ, let me take the example of जहि jahi (loṭ lakāra, second person, singular) from root √han as cited in the Mahābhāṣya. In han+hi, 'han' is replaced with 'ja' by हन्तेर्जः 6.4.36 making it as ja+hi. In this situation, sūtra अतो हेः 6.4.105 teaches the elision of the suffix –hi after 'ja', which is a-ending. Here both the rules 6.4.36 and 6.4.105 have 'ja' as the common āśraya of operation. So, as per rule 6.4.22, the operation of 'ja' replacement by sūtra 6.4.36 is considered as asiddhvat (as if unknown), so the other rule 6.4.105 is prohibited because it sees 'han,' and not 'ja'. Thus, the suffix -hi is not elided.

Similarly, for उत्सर्गलक्षणभावार्थ, let me take the example of शाधि śādhi (loṭ lakāra, second person, singular) from root √śās as cited in Mahābhāṣya. In śās+hi, suffix -hi is replaced with –dhi by sūtra हुझल्भ्यो: हेर्धिः 6.4.101 making it śās + dhi. Here sūtra शा हौ 6.4.35 has to operate to convert śās into śā making the equation śā+dhi. But it can convert śāś into śa only if it is suffixed with –hi pratyaya. As such it cannot operate. Here also both the sūtras हुझल्भ्यो: हेर्धिः 6.4.101 and शा हौ 6.4.35 have the common āśraya of operation. So, as per the present sūtra असिद्धवदत्राभात् 6.4.22, the operation of sūtra हुझल्भ्यो: हेर्धिः 6.4.101 converting suffix –hi into –dhi will be considered as asiddhvat (unknown) to the utsarga rule शा हौ 6.4.35, which will be allowed to operate converting śās into śā and making the form śādhi.

In both the examples cited in the Mahābhāṣtya, the rules have been considered as asiddhvat and not asiddha, although the process of asiddhvat is denoted by the term asiddha itself. I quote the concerned discussion of Mahābhāṣya hereunder for the perusal of the student.

असिद्धवदत्राभात् (6.4.22) असिद्धवचनं किमर्थम् ? असिद्धवचनप्रयोजनवार्तिकम् ॥ १ ॥) - असिद्धवचने उक्तम् - किमुक्तम् । तत्र

तावदुक्तम्। षत्वतुकोरसिद्धवचनमादेशलक्षणप्रतिषेधार्थमुत्सर्गलक्षणभावार्थं इति । इहापि - असिद्धवचनमादेशलक्षणप्रतिषेधार्थमुत्सर्गलक्षणभावार्थं च । तत्र - आदेशलक्षणप्रतिषेधार्थं तावत् - आगहि, जहि । गतं, गतवानिति । अनुनासिकलोपे जभावे च कृते अतो लोपः 6.4.48 अतो हेः (6.4.105) इति च प्राप्नोति । असिद्धत्वान्न भवति । उत्सर्गलक्षणभावार्थं च - एधि, शाधीति । अस्तिशास्त्योरेत्वशाभावयोः कृतयोर्झल्लक्षणं धित्वं न प्राप्नोति । असिद्धत्वाद्भवति।

asiddhavadatrābhāt (6.4.22) asiddhavachanaṁ kimartham ? asiddhavachanaprayojanavārtikam // 1 //) - asiddhavachane uktam - kimuktam / tatra tāvaduktam / ṣatvatukorasiddhavachanamādeśalakṣaṇapratiṣedhārthamu tsargalakṣaṇabhāvārthaṁ iti / ihāpi - asiddhavachanamādeśalakṣaṇapratiṣedhārthamutsargalakṣa ṇabhāvārthaṁ cha / tatra - ādeśalakṣaṇapratiṣedhārthaṁ tāvat - āgahi, jahi / gataṁ, gatavāniti / anunāsikalope jabhāve cha kṛte ato lopaḥ 6.4.48 ato heḥ (105) iti cha prāpnoti / asiddhatvānna bhavati / utsargalakṣaṇabhāvārthaṁ cha - ēdhi, śādhīti / astiśāstyoretvaśābhāvayoḥ kṛtayorjhallakṣaṇaṁ dhitvaṁ na prāpnoti / asiddhatvādbhavati /

I very much appreciate the meaning of asiddhavat given by the student as equal to kāryāsiddhi. (p.181). Here it may also be remembered that Pāṇinian tradition takes the term 'asiddha' both for śāstrāsiddha and kāryāsiddha, as already discussed above. Here the term asiddha used by tradition to denote asiddhavat should be taken for the meaning of kāryāsiddha as per context.

From the foregoing discussion, it is crystal clear that the Indian grammatical tradition developed over the last many thousands of years is on the right track. The student could not understand its intricacies because of ignorance. So, developed a hypothesis suggesting the traditional interpretation of Pāṇini's sūtras is wrong, and proposing a new interpretation that is actually wrong. We should not forget that Pāṇini composed his grammar by consulting many schools of grammar prior to him; he also taught his grammar to his students. But with the passage of time, after Pāṇini, many doubts and many views became prevalent by the time Patañjali, so he had to write the Mahābhāṣya to address all views and doubts that were haunting the scholars during his time.

Let me also allude that all post-Pāṇinian scholars, who developed prakriyā (derivational) system based upon Pāṇini's grammar, remained confined to the boundary lines drawn by Pāṇini. But the student crossed that boundary line. I accept he has a fertile mind, but his intelligence potential could not be utilized properly for want of good supervision. He did not find a good Guru who could restrain him from being misled owing to confusions. Pāṇini's algorithm had never been a riddle; it is a riddle for the student and many others who are not able to understand it from the proper perspective. His whole thesis needs revision.

Although the above analysis is sufficient to expose the student, yet here onward the reply to the thesis will be given by Rajveer Arya, a serious student of Pāṇini's grammar, analysing the examples quoted by the student and referring to new examples that will help expose the veracity and authenticity of the hypothesis of the student.

Chapter-2

Discerning Cambridge Thesis

Rishi Raj Popat proclaimed that his ingenuious method is capable of dealing with Aṣṭādhyāyī more effectively than that of traditional and modern approaches. To establish his hypothesis, he has built up his premises on an assumption that traditional and modern vyākaraṇa approaches failed to decipher the actual meaning and role of the following two sūtras:

विप्रतिषेधे परं कार्यम् (1.4.2)

यस्मात् प्रत्ययविधिस्तदादि प्रत्ययेऽङ्गम् (1.4.13)

He even questioned the veracity and understanding of traditionalist and modern vyākarṇāchāryas with reference to following three sūtras: -

1. षत्वतुकोरसिद्धः (6.1.86)
2. 'असिद्धवदत्राभात्' (6.4.22)
3. 'पूर्वत्रासिद्धम्' (8.2.1)

Going forward the student challenged brilliance of ancient Ṛṣis and tried to deride their mental faculty in understanding applicability of:

1. अलोऽन्तस्य (1.151)
2. ङिच्च (1.1.52)
3. आदेः परस्य (1.1.53)
4. अनेकाल्शित् सर्वस्य (1.1.54)
5. अलोऽन्त्यात् पूर्व उपधा (1.1.64)
6. तस्मिन्निति निर्दिष्टे पूर्वस्य (1.1.65)

7. दीर्घात् पदान्ताद् वा (6.1.73)

In order to prove his postulation, he came up with a maxim with the name Same-Step Rule Interaction, acronym SSRI. This consists of two rules

1) Same operand Interaction (SOI)-Type-1 and

2) Different operand Interaction (DOI)-Type-2.

On the basis of diagrammatical representation, he conjectured the concept of unidirectional blocking, mutual blocking, or non-blocking of different sūtras.

For a better understanding of readers, we are providing a conceptual understanding of his conjectured concept in short:

* A+B; here A and B are two operands akin to प्रकृति (A) + प्रत्यय (B) interaction.
* When two sūtras let 'a' and 'b' interact with operand A and B respectively then it is treated as DOI operation i.e. A (a) + B (b).
* When two sūtras let 'a' and 'b' interact with the same operand viz either with A or B then it is treated as SOI operation i.e. A (a, b) or B (a, b).

Subsequently, he has drawn the following conclusions:

- 'विप्रतिषेधे परं कार्यम्' sūtra is only meant for DOI operations
- In SOI operation when there is mutual blocking or unidirectional blocking then a more specific rule wins

Besides the above-proposed assumption, he has developed new structure of SOI-L and SOI-M to deal with nominal inflection (नामरूप) and sandhi (सन्धि) derivations respectively.

In his exposition, the scholar has alluded to the operation of sañjñā sūtras at point no 1.6 under chapter-1 and also about sūtras of metarule (परिभाषा) at page no. 219. However, by and large he has overlooked the interaction of sañjñā sūtras which decide qualification for interaction of प्रकृति and प्रत्यय, i.e., धातु, प्रातिपादिक, सार्वधातुक, आर्धधातुक, कृत्, etc. In case of simultaneous interaction of two or more sañjñā sūtras at the same operand, which sañjñā will gain precedence has not been delved in. However, from the arguments presented and assumptions made at relevant topics, it is apparent that the thesis deals with sañjñā sūtras in accordance with SOI, DOI principles.

Does this claim hold water and can pass the litmus test of Ārṣa-vidhi or is it just another attempt to discredit the veracity of Indian Ṛṣis at the behest of some of the faculties of the University?

In the forthcoming chapter, viz. chapter-4, I will briefly present the fallacy and reasons for the failure of this tall claim. Besides, in chapter-7 and chapter-8, I will indicate the problems with his hypothesis vis-à-vis Ārṣa-vidhi.

Hence-forth, the methodology of thesis submitted to Cambridge University will be denoted as C-process.

Chapter - 3

Dispelling the Myth of C-process

विप्रतिषेधे परं कार्यं (1.4.2)

समर्थः पादविधिः (2.1.1), Maharishi Dayanand interpret and elucidate this sūtra in the light of Maharshi Patanjali's Mahābhāṣya. His exposition of this sūtra in Vedāṅga Prakāśais is as follows:

"...जो कुछ इस व्याकरणशास्त्र में पद को विधानकार्य सुना जाता है, वह समर्थ को जानना चाहिये।

व्याकरण में प्रथम यही परिभाषा सर्वत्र प्रवृत होती है, क्योंकि "अपदं न प्रयुञ्जीत" – अपद अर्थात् सुप् तिङ् प्रत्यय से रहित शब्द का प्रयोग कभी न करना चाहिये। और सुप् और तिङ् भी समर्थ ही से विधान होते हैं असमर्थ से नहीं, क्योंकी बिना संज्ञा के सामर्थ्य नहीं होता, सामर्थ्य से बिना उससे प्रत्यय की उत्पत्ति नहीं हो सकती, और इसके विना प्रयोग भी नहीं बन सकता। क्योंकिः –

"न केवला प्रकृतिः प्रयोक्तव्या न च केवलः प्रत्ययः। प्रकृति प्रत्ययौ प्रत्ययार्थं सह ब्रूतः" ।।

इस महाभाष्य के वचन का अभिप्राय यही है कि दोनों के मिलें बिना कोइ भी कार्य सिद्ध नहीं हो सकता। इस कारण सामर्थ्य से [के] बिना किसी प्रत्ययकार्य वा कोई व्याकरण की बात पृथक् **नहीं हो सकती**। इसलिये इसी सूत्र के भाष्य में –

परिभाषायां च सत्यां यावान् व्याकरणे पदगन्धो नाम स सर्वः संगृहीतो भवति।। (महाभाष्य 2.1.1)

यह परिभाषा सूत्र है। इस लिये जो कुछ व्याकरण का विषय है, उस सब में इस सूत्र की प्रवृत्ति अवश्य होती है,.." (Sandhi Viṣayaḥ)

It implies that whatever is stated in the vyākaraṇa rules about padas should be accomplished with the समर्थ (qualified). Everywhere in the vyākaraṇa this definition

(2.1.1) is to be applied first because base (प्रकृति) without suffix (प्रत्यय) can never be used. Sup (सुप) and tiṅ (तिङ्) are also prescribed on the strength of their being qualified because, without sañjñākaraṇa (naming), prakṛtis or pratyayas are not legally qualified to act as operands and hence no pada can be formed. Paribhāṣā quoted by Patañjali in his Mahābhāṣya also stipulates that whatever the subject or topic of vyākaraṇa be, this sūtra (2.1.1) has to be applied mandatorily everywhere.

"पदविधि समर्थ के आश्रित होती है। समर्थ अर्थात् जिसके साथ जिसकी योग्यता हो, उसी के साथ उसका पदकार्य्य होता है।....

...जैसे-'भू+तव्यत्', यहां धातुसञ्ज्ञा के विना 'भू' शब्द प्रत्ययविधान में असमर्थ तथा तव्यत् यह कृत और प्रत्ययसञ्ज्ञा के विना विधान होने ही में असमर्थ है। इसी प्रकार सर्वत्र समझना चाहिये।

..व्याकरण में सब सूत्रों से प्रथम इस सूत्र की प्रवृत्ति होती है, त्तपश्चात्...."(Naamik)

It implies that pada operation is dependent upon samarthas (qualified constituents). Once a constituent is qualified (समर्थ) with respect to another, it will go with the concerned constituent to act as an operand for pada operation. As in the case of भू+तव्यत्, unless भू is qualified to be a dhātu and तव्यत् is qualified to be a pratyaya, cannot act as operand for pada-operation. This sūtra assigning sañjñā is first applied in the grammar.

Let us understand above stated definition by the following examples:

Kindly note that in the following examples for the sake of brevity, we have avoided discussion about the process of assigning प्रातिपदिक, धातु, विभक्ति, एकवचन etc sañjñās.

राम+भिस्	राम+भिस् acquires पद sañjñā by sūtra सुप्तिङन्तम् पदम् (1.4.14) राम acquires पद sañjñā by sūtra स्वादिष्वसर्वनामस्थाने (1.4.17) राम acquires अङ्ग sañjñā by sūtra यस्मात् प्रत्ययविधिस्तदादि प्रत्ययेऽङ्गम् (1.4.13)
वाच्+भिस्	वाच्+भिस् acquires पद sañjñā by sūtra सुप्तिङन्तम् पदम् (1.4.14) वाच् acquires पद sañjñā by sūtra स्वादिष्वसर्वनामस्थाने (1.4.17) वाच् acquires अङ्ग sañjñā by sūtra यस्मात् प्रत्ययविधिस्तदादि प्रत्ययेऽङ्गम् (1.4.13)
भू+तस्	भू+तस् acquires पद sañjñā by sūtra सुप्तिङन्तम् पदम् (1.4.14) भू acquires अङ्ग sañjñā by sūtra यस्मात् प्रत्ययविधिस्तदादि प्रत्ययेऽङ्गम् (1.4.13) तस् acquires सार्वधातुक sañjñā by sūtra तिङ् शित सार्वधातुकम् (3.4.113)
भू+शप्+तस्	भ+शप्+तस् acquires पद sañjñā by sūtra सुप्तिङन्तम् पदम् (1.4.14) भू+ शप् acquires अङ्ग sañjñā by sūtra यस्मात् प्रत्ययविधिस्तदादि प्रत्ययेऽङ्गम् (1.4.13) भू acquires अङ्ग sañjñā by sūtra यस्मात् प्रत्ययविधिस्तदादि प्रत्ययेऽङ्गम् (1.4.13) शप् acquires अङ्ग sañjñā by sūtra यस्मात् प्रत्ययविधिस्तदादि प्रत्ययेऽङ्गम् (1.4.13) शप् acquires सार्वधातुक sañjñā by sūtra तिङ् शित सार्वधातुकम् (3.4.113)

तस् acquires सार्वधातुक sañjñā by sūtra तिङ् शित सार्वधातुकम् (3.4.113)

In examples 1 and 2, sūtra 1.4.17 and 1.4.13 are cases of SOI, whereas with regard to sūtra 1.4.14, C-process is silent.

In example 3, sūtra 1.4.13 and 3.4.113 are cases of DOI, whereas with regard to sūtra 1.4.14, C-process is silent.

In example 4, DOI and SOI operations become a complex equation.

If we analyze the aforementioned examples, then the question arises how to decide the sañjñā sūtra is to be applied first?

Unless the applicability of sañjñā sūtra is decided विधि sūtras (metarules) cannot become applicable.

To unravel this perplexing situation, we will have to mandatorily understand sūtra विप्रतिषेधे परं कार्यं (1.4.2) in context of sūtra समर्थः पदविधिः (2.1.1). If we peruse Maharshi Dayanand's explanation, then it becomes clear that Maharshi Pāṇini has conceptualized अष्टाध्यायी sūtras in a way that various derivational processes can be initiated.

Hence, sūtras are arranged in eight chapters, which are subdivided into four pādas. These sūtras are arranged in serial order and that is why the term 'paraṁ' in sūtra विप्रतिषेधे परं कार्यं (1.4.2) refers to the horrizontal placement of sūtras.

However, C-process failed to understand this basic concept and conjectured the meaning of 'paraṁ' in the sūtra विप्रतिषेधे परं कार्यं (1.4.2) as right-hand side operand. This premise has not only cramped the Pāṇinian derivational process but has also proved to be counterproductive.

2. उणादयो बहुलम् (3.3.1)

C-process while delving into the derivation of स्योन: and finding himself in awkward situation, decry उणादि कोष: by following remarks:

> "There is no evidence that Panini has composed the Uṇādi sūtras. Therefore, this derivation, which requires us to add न to श्वि as per उणादि सूत्र (289) is not Paniniyan at all." (Appendix C, example-1, p.230)

The assumption of the thesis is irrefutable proof that the student appropriated his views on the works of occidental Sanskrit grammarians. Otherwise, he would not have made illogical, baseless remarks about उणादि कोष:; this is despite the fact that he has delved into the derivation of भवान् (example-2, p. 86).

Had it been known to the student that भवत् is derived from 'भा' दिप्तौ धातु (verbal base) with डवतुप् pratyaya taught by Uṇādi sūtra भातेर्डवतुप् (उणा-1.63), he would have refrained from copying from foreign sources.

There are many sūtras in अष्टाध्यायी which refer to a derivational form of उणादिकोष:; some of them are listed below:

- जाग्रोऽविचिण्णल्ङित्सु 7.3.85, In this sūtra वि refers to विन् pratyaya of Uṇādikoṣa.
- अत: कृकमिकंसकुम्भपात्रकुशाकर्णीष्वनव्ययस्य 8.3.46 teaches formation of कंस from the root कम्

Maharshi Dayanand, in his Pāribhāṣika, while elaborating on Paribhāṣā-22 by taking the example of sūtra 8.3.46, says "अतः कृकमिकंस, इस सूत्र में कंस शब्द का पाठ व्यर्थ है, क्योंकी उणादि में (कमेः सः) इस सूत्र से 'कम' धातु का कंस शब्द बना है। कम् धातु से सामान्य प्रयोगों के ग्रहण में 'कंस' शब्द का भी ग्रहण हो जाता, फिर कंस शब्द क्यों पढ़ा। इसलिये यह परिभाषा है।

उणादयोऽव्युत्पन्नानि प्रातिपदिकानि।

उणादि प्रातिपदिक अव्युत्पन्न, अर्थात् उन का सर्वत्र प्रकृति, प्रत्यय, कारक आदि से योगिक यथार्थ अर्थ नहीं लगता। अर्थात् उणादि शब्द बहुदा रूढ़ि होता है।"

He further says "इसी प्रकार कंसीयपरशव्ययोर्यञञ् लुक् च (4.3.166) सूत्र में प्रत्ययस्य लुकश्लुलुपः (1.1.61), इस सूत्र से परशव्य शब्द का लुक कहा हुआ उकार प्रत्यय होने से अव्युत्पन्नपक्ष मान के 'परशु' शब्द के उकार का लुक नहीं होता। इत्यादि अनेक प्रयोजन हैं..."

It implies that उणादि are underived forms, which indicates that the meaning of these words is not always derived simply by applying प्रकृति (base), प्रत्यय (suffix), etc. That is why they are generally treated as having a conventional form.

Maharshi Dayanand further clarifies this subject in his Magnum Opus "ऋग्वेदादि-भाष्य-भूमिका", chapter-33, व्याकरणनियमविषयः. While discussing Maharshi Patañjali's Mahābhāṣya with reference to उणादयो० Maharshi Dayanand observes as under:

"इस सूत्र के उपर महाभाष्यकार पतञ्जलि मुनि उणादिपाठ की व्यवस्था बांधते है कि-(बहुलकं०) उणादिपाठ में थोड़े से धातुओं से प्रत्ययविधान किया है, सो बहुल के होने से वे प्रत्यय अन्य धातुओं से भी होते हैं। इसी प्रकार प्रत्यय भी उस ग्रन्थ में थोड़े से नमुने के लिये पढ़े हैं, इनसे अन्य भी नवीन प्रत्यय शब्दों में देखकर समझ लेना चाहिये। जैसे 'ऋफिडः' इस शब्द उणादिगण से ऋ धातु से फिड प्रत्यय समझा जाता है। इसी प्रकार अन्यत्र भी जानना चाहियें। तथा जितने शब्द उणादिगण से सिद्ध होते हैं, उनमें जितने कार्य्य सूत्रों करके होने चाहियें वे सब नहीं होते हैं, सो भी बहुल ही का प्रताप है।

(किं पुनः०) इसमें जो कोई ऐसी शंका करे कि उणादिपाठ में जितने धातुओं से जितने प्रत्यय विधान किये, और जितने कार्य्य शब्दों की सिद्धि में सूत्रों से हो सकते हैं, उनसे अधिक क्यों होते है? तो इसका उत्तर यह है कि (नैगम०) वेदों में जितने शब्द हैं, तथा संसार में असंख्य संज्ञाशब्द हैं, ये सब अच्छी प्रकार सिद्ध नहीं हो सकते, इसलिये पूर्वोक्त तीन प्रकार के कार्य्य बहुलवचन से उणादि में होते हैं। जिसके होने से अनेक प्रकार के हजारह शब्द सिद्ध होते हैं।"

In the above two statements, Maharshi Dayanand has comprehensibly dispelled the doubt and cleared the air. In these statements, he implied that Maharshi Patañjali had made arrangements for उणादिपाठ. In उणादिपाठ, suffixes have been prescribed with few dhātus; these pratyayas (suffixes) variously (बहुल) operate with other dhātus to derive words, i.e., can be added to other dhātus to which they are not prescribed. In the same way, few pratyayas are prescribed in the उणादिकोष on a sample basis, so as per requirement, more words can be derived with the help of Uṇādi suffixes. As in the case of ऋफिडः, we can understand the presence of फिड pratyaya. Similarly, elsewhere same process should be applied. Many a time, in all the words derived with the help of उणादि suffixes, the operations taught by sūtra are not applicable; this is also due to बहुल (various) application.

If someone doubts about more derivational operations of pratyayas with dhātu than prescribed in उणादिपाठ, the answer is that in the Vedas and conventional practice, we have innumerable vocables in use, all of which can't be derived through established norms; hence aforementioned three types of operations are taught in उणादि through बहुल application. Because of this, myriad numbers of words can be derived.

Maharshi Dayanand further states:

यह सब ऋषियों का प्रबन्ध इसलिये है कि शब्दसागर अथाह है, इसकी थाह

व्याकरण से नहीं मिल सकती। जो कहें कि ऐसा व्यकारण क्यों नहीं बनाया कि जिससे शब्दसागर के पार पहुंच जाते, तो यह समझना कि कितने ही पोथा बनाते और जन्म-जन्मान्तरों भर पढ़ते, तो भी पार होना दुर्लभ हो जाता। इसलिये यह सब पूर्वोक्त प्रबन्ध ऋषियों ने किया है, जिससे शब्दों की व्यवस्था मालूम हो जाय।

That is, the system of बहुल (various) application is introduced by Ṛṣis because words are innumerable, which cannot be derived with the vyākaraṇa alone. If someone asks why such a vyākaraṇa is not composed as could have encompassed an entire ocean of words? Then it may be known that in spite of the creation of voluminous works and assiduous reading through various life cycles, it would have been challenging task to govern all words. That is why Ṛṣis have made this arrangement, to make it convenient to comprehend the derivation of words.

Chapter- 4

Reasons for the Failure of C-process

In this chapter, we will briefly discuss the weakness and drawbacks of the C-process. Besides, we will also indicate why Ārṣa-vidhi gains supremacy over C-process.

The reasons for the failure of the DOI/ SOI:

1. In chapter six of the thesis working with nominal inflection of 'देव' an attempt has been made to claim the discernment of Pāṇini's methodology and in chapter-2 at page no. 50 'देवैः' has been projected to establish the integrity of SSRI/SOI/DOI maxim. But, in the excitement of deriding acumen of Indian Ṛṣis, the thesis turned a blind eye to the following sūtras:

   i. बहुलं छन्दसि (7.1.10), this sūtra derives both देवेभिः and देवैः

   ii. नेदमदसोरकोः (7.1.11), this sura derives एभिः अमीभिः instead of ऐः and अदैः

   ii. Vārttika "जसादिषु च्छन्दसि वावचनं प्राङ् णौ चङ्युपधायाः" that supplement Aṣṭādhāyī and assist in deriving both अग्न्यः and अग्नयः in Vedic usage.

Besides aforementioned sūtras and vārttika, there are other sūtras which proves futility of SSRI/SOI/DOI maxim and supports ancient, traditional Ārṣa-vidhi method of पूर्व से पर, पर से नित्य, नित्य से अन्तरङ्ग and अन्तरङ्ग से अपवाद is powerful.

2. The newly invented C-process, in many places, instead of simplifying the derivation, makes it more

cumbersome. This becomes evident starting from example no. 3 of chapter 2, dealing with the derivation of "वारि+टा." The traditional Ārṣa-vidhi derives वारिणा by following the simplified principle of "परत्व और अपवाद, but C-process fails to simplify the derivation. Instead, it gets into cumbersome process of juxtaposing and eliminating sandhi sūtra इको यणचि (6.1.74) and नुम् आगम् sūtra इकोऽचि विभक्तौ (7.1.73) with respect to आङो नास्त्रियाम् (7.3.119). Despite accepting the difficulty posed by the newly invented C-process, the thesis quotes Bālamanorama to prove its veracity.

3. C-process is at a loss while defining the applicability of ह्रस्वनद्यापो नुट् (7.1.54) and इदितो नुम् धातोः (7.1.58) in case of nominal inflection of neuter gender, genitive plural. It glossed over the following fact:

- From sūtra आमि सर्वनाम्नः सुट् (7.1.52) anuvṛtti of आमि goes up to 7.1.57 and ह्रस्वनद्यापो नुट् (7.1.54) falls under the jurisdiction of this anuvṛtti.
- From sūtra इदितो नुम् धातोः (7.1.58) anuvṛtti of नुम् goes up to 7.1.83 and इकोऽचि विभक्तौ (7.1.73) falls under the jurisdiction of this anuvṛtti.

Due to the above-stated position, while deriving वारि+औ, वारि+जस् et al. of neuter gender nominal base, the इकोऽचि विभक्तौ (7.1.73) teaches the application of नुम् - augment, as sūtra 7.1.73 falls within anuvṛtti of 7.1.58 and is also specific to neuter gender.

In deriving neuter gender, the genitive plural of वारि+आम्, because of the aforementioned condition of नुम् augment, is applicable here. However, if we apply नुम्, then it will be affixed to the last vowel of वारि, and then elongation (दीर्घत्व) of the last vowel of वारि will not take place leading to the wrong derivation.

If we apply ह्रस्वनद्यापो नुट् (7.1.54) then also it is blocked by इकोऽचि विभक्तौ (7.1.73) on two grounds, one it being specific to neuter gender by virtue of anuvṛtti and lastly it is पर sūtra to ह्रस्वनद्यपो नुट् (7.1.54). Hence, vārttika नुमचिरतृज्वद्भावेभ्यो नुट् पूर्वविप्रतिषेधेन resolves this issue by making नुट् applicable and thus arriving at correct form वारीणाम्. But C-process belittled vārttika without acknowledging the factual position.

4. In the case of derivation of क्रोष्टु+आम्, C-process failed to take into account the following facts:

- Sūtra विभाषा तृतीयादिष्वचि (7.1.97) is applicable alternatively/optionally. The non-application option is called निषेध पक्ष.
- Therefore, in derivational operations of क्रोष्टु + टा etc, when sūtra 7.1.97 is applied, then we derive क्रोष्ट्रा and in निषेध पक्ष, we get क्रोदुना.
- Similarly in the case of क्रोष्टु+आम् because of परत्व and also being specific both the forms i.e., क्रोष्टृ and क्रोष्टु (निषेध पक्ष) are achieved. And, in both the cases sūtra ह्रस्वनद्यापो नुट् (7.1.54) is applicable, but vārttika नुमचिरतृज्वद्भावेभ्यो नुट् पूर्वविप्रतिषेधेन resolves the issue by giving precedence to ह्रस्वनद्यापो नुट् (7.1.54) and restricting application of विभाषा तृतीयादिष्वचि (7.1.97).

5. C-process indulges in the burdensome process of grid mechanism of sandhi derivations, as promulgated by the Laghu-Siddhānta Kaumudī. On analysis of the process adopted by C-process, it becomes apparent that it is oblivious to the 7 processes of Ārṣa-vidhi essential for understanding the sūtras. The 7 processes are:

I. Padaccheda

II. Vibhakti Vachan

III. Samāsa (compound words)

IV. Aadhikāra/anuvṛtti

V. Artha

VI. Udāharaṇa.

VII. Siddhi

If the understanding of the above-referred processes had been there, then C-process could have acknowledged and known the following facts:

- Adhikāra of संहितायाम् (6.1.70) goes upto 6.1.151.
- Anuvṛtti of अचि in sūtra इको यणचि (6.1.74) goes upto 6.1.120.
- Adhikāra of एकः पूर्वपरयोः (6.1.81) goes upto 6.1.107
- Anuvṛtti of आद् in sūtra आद् गुणः (6.1.84) goes upto 6.1.93.
- Sūtras आद् गुणः (6.1.84), वृद्धिरेचि (7.1.85) and अकःसवर्णे दीर्घः (6.1.102) operates under jurisdiction of adhikāra and anuvṛtti of 6.1.151, 6.1.74 and 6.1.81.
- The संज्ञा and परिभाषा sūtras वृद्धिरादैच (1.1.1), अदेङ् गुणः (1.1.2), इको गुणवृद्धि (1.1.3) and तुल्यास्यप्रयत्नं सवर्णम् (1.1.9) defines आ, औ, ऐ as वृद्धि; अ, ओ, ए as गुण; गुण, वृद्धि operations to be done within jurisdiction of इक् प्रत्यहार and following pairs of vowels are सवर्ण, viz. अ and आ; इ and ई; उ and ऊ; ऋ and ऌ.

Discernment of the aforesaid Ārṣa-vidhi principle would have made sandhi operations, dealt with in the thesis, more fruitful and comprehensible. Instead of performing the C-process's complex operation of juxtaposing different sūtras, the Ārṣa-vidhi method achieves the desired result as under:

* राम + औदारय

औ is वृद्धि sound and followed by अ of राम, hence वृद्धिरेचि (7.1.85) sūtra, being पर and अपवाद, is applied.

* तव + आनन्दम्

अ of तव and आ of आनन्दम् are सवर्ण, hence अकःसवर्णे दीर्घः (6.1.102), being पर and अपवाद, is applied.

* भानु + उदय, here also उ+उ are सवर्ण, hence अकःसवर्णे दीर्घः (6.1.102), being पर and अपवाद, is applied.

6. Some Aṣṭādhyāyī sūtras are not easily discernable. In that situation, योग विभाग is done to make them more coherent and understandable without changing the arrangement of sūtras. Maharshi Patañjali in the Māhābāaṣhya did योग विभाग of औदच्च घेः (7.3.118) into औत् and अच्च घेः and derived anuvṛtti of इदुद्भ्याम् (7.3.117) with औत् only. Subsequently, Maharshi Patañjali arrived at the same conclusion by treating औदच्च घेः as one sūtra.

But, C-process blindly followed western vyākraṇāchāryas in refuting योग विभाग process. From the content of the thesis, it is perceptible that western vyākarṇāchāryas failed to understand the Mahābhāṣya. In their efforts to set aside the method of Mahābhāṣya, they welded two sūtras 7.3.117 and 118 into one, i.e., इदुद्भ्याम् औदच्च घेः.

C-process during derivation of वारी+ङि (neuter locative) expressed its concurrence with this methodology but failed to explain how the scope of

इदुद्भ्याम् be determined with reference to ङेराम् नद्याम्नीभ्यः (7.3.116) and औदच्च घे (7.3.118). If we accept this amalgamation, then derivation of पत्यौ, सख्यौ will be beyond the scope of this sūtra.

It is pertinient to note that methodolgy of योग विभाग is visible at many places, for example, sūtra कृते ग्रन्थे (4.3.116), संज्ञायाम् (4.3.117), कुलालादिभ्यो वुञ् (4.3.118), अज्झनगमां सनि (6.4.16) etc.

7. The C-process' principle of SOI, DOI falls apart while dealing with the derivation of त्रि+आम्, masculine, genitive plural form. Finding itself in an awkward situation, C-process questioned the sequential order of sūtras from 7.1.50 to 7.1.57 and pointed to oddly placed sūtra त्रेस्त्रयः (7.1.53).

To justify its proposition, the thesis started concocting historical Sanskrit grammar, and mythological stories disseminated by western historians, which has been aptly dismembered by Pt. Yudhisthir Mimanshak ji in his popular work "संस्कृत व्याकरण शास्त्र का इतिहास" written in three volumes.

C-process conjectured that if ever Maharshi Pāṇini wanted to derive त्रयाणाम्, then he would have come up with sūtra त्रेस्त्रयः नामि, almost similar into नामि (6.4.3). But it missed two points while conceiving this vulnerable premise:

I. There are many words and usages in ancient Vedic literature which Maharshi Pāṇini despite, extraordinary genius, could not encompass under the derivational machine of Aśṭādhyāyī. Kātyāyana, through his vārttikas, has pointed out to many such usages. For more details, one may refer to

"संस्कृत व्याकरण शास्त्र का इतिहास". There are various Vedic vocables, प्रत्यय and धातु which are not covered by Maharshi Pāṇini in his upadeśas (texts). For more detail, one may refer to the Ṛgvedādi Bhāṣya Bhūmikā of Maharshi Dayanand Saraswati.

II. C-process while postulating formation of sūtra त्रेस्त्रयः नामि failed to acknowledge the fact that this sūtra will become अपवाद sūtra to त्रिचतुरोः स्त्रियां तिसृचतसृ (7.2.99). Besides, त्रि acting as स्थानिवत्, will not allow the formation of तिसृणाम् and thus rendering Pāṇiniyan derivational method ineffective.

8. In the derivation of भवान्, the C-process finding itself in an unpropitious situation and sticking to the fatal disposition of not accepting the unparalleled acumen of Ārṣa-vidhi, came up with the fabricated illogical conclusion.

In this attempt, thesis dreamed of मण्डूकप्लुति न्याय and urged मण्डूकप्लूति गति of संयोगस्य from sūtra सान्तमतः संयोगस्य (6.4.10) to अत्वसन्तस्य चाधातोः (6.4.14) and associated संयोगस्य with अतु of sūtra 6.4.14. To justify its raison d'etre, thesis cites presence of चासम्बुद्धौ from 6.4.8 into sūtra सौ च (6.4.13) as a case of मण्डूकप्लुति गति. But, C-process failed to justify its rationale.

However, here we are highlighting a few tickling points which appear to be more plausible than C-process's proposed solution:

- सान्त is लुप्तषष्ठयान्त in sūtra 6.4.10 and if संयोगस्य can jump to sūtra 6.4.14 then why can't अतु be placed with 6.4.10 instead of 6.4.14 ?

  This logic will render brevity to sūtra 6.4.14 as असन्तस्य and sūtra 6.4.10 will be read as अतुसान्तमहतः

संयोगस्य, which will serve the purpose.

- In Sūtra 6.4.14 अत्वसान्तस्य has द्वन्द्वगर्भबहुव्रीहि समास, as such how can संयोगस्य be associated with अतु? Instead, if अतु is placed at 6.4.10 then this problem too will be overcomed.

If we go by the newly conjectured hypothesis, then we will find that the derivational system of Pāṇini is fraught with more problems than solutions.

Instead of going into details, I am discussing a few important points which were missed in the thesis while speculating on modality and working of anuvṛtti and मण्डूकप्लुति न्याय. In this process, the author miserably acted beyond the purview of Paṇini's vyākaraṇa system.

- Sūtra अत्वसन्तस्य चाधातोः (6.4.14) falls under the jurisdiction of adhikāra and anuvṛttis of the following sutras:
    - From ढ्रलोपे पूर्वस्य दीर्घोऽणः (6.3.110), anuvṛtti of दीर्घ extends up to 6.4.18
    - Adhikāra of अङ्गस्य (6.4.1) continues up to 7.4.97
    - From नोपधायाः (6.4.7), anuvṛtti of उपधायाः continues up to 6.4.18
    - From सर्वनामस्थाने चासम्बुद्धौ (6.4.8), anuvṛtti of असम्बुद्धौ continues up to 6.4.14
    - सौ च (6.4.13): Anuvṛtti of सौ from this sūtra extends up to 6.4.14
- The scope of anuvṛtti is defined by the following Paribhāṣās as:
    - एकयोगनिर्दिष्टानां सह वा प्रवृत्तिः सह वा निवृत्तिः।।

(Paribhāṣa no. 17)

अर्थात् जो एक सूत्र में निर्देश किये पद हैं, उनकी अन्य सूत्रों में एक साथ प्रवृत्ति और निवृत्ति हो जाती है। इससे (उश्च 1.2.12) सूत्र में 'लिङः सिच' की भी अनुवृत्ति आ जाती है।

It implies that the anuvṛtti of all words connected with an operation read in a particular sūtra, may also continue or discontinue collectively to the following sūtra. For example anuvṛtti of all words read in लिङ्गिचावात्मनेपदेषु (1.2.11) continue to (उश्च 1.2.12).

- एकयोगनिर्दिष्टानामप्येकदेशानुवृत्तिर्भवति।।(Paribhāṣā no 18)

  अर्थात् एक सूत्र में पृथक पठित पदों में भी कहीं एकदेश की अनुवृत्ति होती है। इसी प्रकार अन्यत्र बहुत स्थलों के सूत्र वार्तिकों में यह रीति दिख पड़ती है, कि जैसे कहीं दो पदों की अनुवृत्ति आती है, उनमें से जब एक को छोड़ना होता है तब द्वितीय पद को फिर से पढ़ते हैं। तो यही प्रयोजन है कि दोनों पदों की अनुवृत्ति एक साथ ही चलती है उसमें से एक को छोड़ के दूसरे पद की अनुवृत्ति नहीं जा सकती ।।17।।

  इस से उत्तरपदाधिकार का पादपर्यन्त जाना सिद्ध हो गया तथा (दामहायनान्ताच्च 4.1.27) यहां पूर्व सूत्र से 'संख्या' की अनुवृत्ति आती है, और 'अव्यय' की नहीं ।।18।।

  It implies that the anuvṛtti of one word from many words connected with an operation read in a particular sūtra, may also continue to the subsequent sūtra in. For example, anuvṛtti of one word संख्या from sūtra संख्याव्ययादेर्ङीप् 4.1.26, continues to the subsequent sūtra दामहायनान्ताच्च 4.1.27, although both संख्या and अव्यय read in sūtra 4.1.26 are connected with the same operation.

From the above description, it is also evident that anuvṛtti of असम्बुद्धौ continues up to 6.4.14. In the sūtras where the anuvṛtti of some word makes its operation redundant, then that anuvṛtti is not read to avoid the redundancy of the operation.

We have a similar example of anuvṛtti of अचि of sūtra इको यणचि (6.1.74), in sandhi operation, which continues up to 6.1.120. In the intermittent sūtras, where अचि is rendered redundant by the presence of other words, it is not read. For example, we may refer the following sūtras:

वृद्धिरेचि (6.1.85), अमि पूर्वः (6.1.103), एङ् पदान्तादति (6.1.105), etc.

- In prathmāvṛtti while explaining anuvṛtti of 'इति' from the sūtra "न वेति विभाषा" (1.1.43) to sūtra "अदर्शनं लोपः" (1.1.59), मण्डूकप्लुति न्याय is defined as "मण्डूकप्लुति न्याय यह है कि जैसे मण्डूक कूद कूद कर चलता है, सरक सरक कर नहीं, इसी प्रकार इस सूत्र में इति पद भी बीच के सूत्रों में न बैठकर यहाँ उपस्थित हुआ"

  Anuvṛtti by virtue of मण्डूकप्लुति न्याय is the continuation of a word from a preceding sūtra to the following sūtra or sūtras in the manner of a frog by skipping one or more sūtras in the middle.

- In Aṣṭādhyāyī, we come across plenty of examples where anuvṛtti of words from preceding sūtra continue to the following sūtra or sūtras by skipping one or more sūtras in the middle. Few of them are listed here: anuvṛtti of त्यदादि from sūtra 7.2.102 to sūtra तदोः सः सावनन्त्ययोः (7.2.105); anuvṛtti of अनुदात्तोपदेशः from sūtra 6.4.37 to sūtra जनसनखनां सञ्झलोः (6.4.42); anuvṛtti of पदान्तात् from sūtra 8.4.41 to sūtra यरोऽनुनासिकेऽनासिको वा (8.4.44), etc.

From the points discussed above it is apparent that Rishi Raj Popat lacks understanding of the function of anuvṛtti by virtue of मण्डूकप्लुति न्याय. Besides, he has wrongly quoted anuvṛtti of चासम्बुद्धौ in place of सम्बुद्धौ, which is a manifestation of his ignorance.

For the derivation of भवान्, see chapter no. 6, आख्यातिक् section, example 22.

9. C-process has done derivation of प्रतीचः (प्रति+अञ्चु+ङस्), genitive form, without assigning tenable reason. It proceeded with the derivation by ignoring the following facts:

"न केवला प्रकृतिः प्रोक्तव्या न च केवलः प्रत्ययः। प्रकृति प्रत्ययौ प्रत्ययार्थं सह ब्रुतः"

This statement of Mahābhāṣya implies that प्रकृति and प्रत्यय in isolation cannot do anything, unless they are united. Without being qualified, no pada can participate in the formation of words. Hence समास, तद्धित operations can take place between qualified प्रातिपदिक and प्रत्यय.

"कृद् ग्रहणे गतिकारकपूर्वस्यापि ग्रहणं भवति।" (Paribhāṣā-28)

"गतिकारकोपपदानां कृद्भिः सह समाकनचनं प्राक सुबुत्पत्तेः।" (Paribhāṣā-66)

In short, the aforementioned paribhāṣās state that गति, कारक and उपपद in the company of कृदन्त suffixes form समास (compound) when followed by सु, etc. pratyayas.

However, C-process straight away started with प्रति+अच्+ङस्, in violation of the above principle without ascribing any reason. In our derivation of सांकूटीनाम we have discussed the problem posed by C-process and have also provided a solution through Ārṣa-vidhi. However, C-process, in part, fortuitously followed Ārṣa-vidhi.

It is pertinent to note that Pāṇini sūtra अचः (6.4.138) unequivocally teaches that the अकार of the word अच् that occurs at the end of a भसंज्ञक अङ्ग is omitted if this 'अच्' happens to be derived from the धातु अञ्चु (गतौ), on account of elision of न् of अञ्च by 6.4.24. Due to this reason, the operation of sūtra 6.4.138 is अपवाद of इको यणचि (6.1.74), and therefore, it applies here. For derivation, see chapter no. 6, तद्धित् section, example-1.

10. In the derivation of सेदुषः (सद्+वस्+ङस्) methodology adopted by C-process is questionable and it also exposes its limitations. Here, two sūtras वसोः सम्प्रसारणम् (6.4.131) and वस्वेकाजाद्घसाम् (7.2.67) are applicable. C-process unilaterally treats sūtra 6.4.131 to be more specific than 7.2.67 without assigning any plausible reason.

On closely examining, it is apparent that both the sūtras are specific to क्वसु pratyaya. But it can be argued that सद् dhātu is अनिट्; hence, sūtra 7.2.67 is more specific than sūtra 6.4.131. However, this reasoning and counter-reasoning leads to an impasse.

From the method followed by C-process, it is evident that in order to align with the final form, C-process has given its conclusion without any logical reasoning.

Ārṣa-vidhi is more cogent and lucid in its derivational method and understanding of Pāṇinian system. Below mentioned principle and Paribhāṣā corroborates our conclusion.

Sūtra वचिस्वपियजादीनां किति (6.1.15) and ग्रहिज्यावयिव्यधिवष्टिविचतिवृश्चतिपृच्छतिभृज्जतीनां ङति च (6.1.16) teaches सम्प्रसारण, but sūtra लिट्यभ्यासस्योभयेषाम् (6.1.17) teaches सम्प्रसारण of अभ्यास् after duplication (द्वित्व). Thus, it is implied that sūtras 6.1.15 and 6.1.16 in normal course teach सम्प्रसारण operation to be performed before द्वित्व operation.

Therefore, in view of above-stated position Paribhāṣā-106 states:

"सम्प्रसारणं सम्प्रसारणाश्रयं च कार्यं बलीयो भवति" means operation of सम्प्रसारण or operation induced by सम्प्रसारण gain precedence being more powerful.

Hence, while deriving सद्+वस्+ङस्, sūtra 6.4.131 gain precedence and override 7.2.64, as such सम्प्रसारण operations block इड् आगम्.

11. C-process derivational method loses its credibility while deriving गर्गाः (गर्गस्य गोत्रापत्यानि बहूनि, many grandsons of Garga), example-3 and गार्गीयाः (गर्गाणाम् छात्राः), example 5 of the thesis (p. 97 & 101).

In the case of गर्गाः, it rejected the form गार्ग्य+जस् derived by Laghu-Siddhanta-Kaumudi and started operation with गर्ग+यञ्+जस्.

Contrary to the derivation of गर्गाः, in the case of derivation of गार्गीयाः from the nominative plural of "गार्ग्य", it started operation with गार्ग्य+छ+जस्, instead of गर्ग+यञ्+आम् (जस्) without ascribing any reason for this deviation. This has landed the C-process into self-created anomaly and also proves that it is another rudimentary method influenced by Siddhānta-Kaumudī and hence fraught with problems already faced by Siddhānta-Kaumdi's students.

Let us understand the problem with C-process:

- Sūtra यञञोश्च (2.4.64) is applicable in the case of plural form only.
- Regarding sūtra गोत्रेऽलगचि (4.1.89), Maharshi

Dayanand explains, "जो 'यास्कादिभ्यो गोत्रे' इत्यादि सूत्रों से जिन गोत्र प्रत्ययों का लुक कह चुके हैं सो न हो, प्राग्दीव्यतीय अजादि प्रत्यय परे हो तो।"

It implies that sūtra 4.1.89 is applicable only in those cases where लुक of गोत्र pratyaya has been done.

- In the derivational form of गार्ग्य+छ+जस्, गार्ग्य is a singular form where the application of 2.4.64 is not possible because sūtra 2.4.64 is taught for the plural form.
- Since sūtra 2.4.64 is not applicable to 'गार्ग्य+छ+जस्,' hence application of sūtra 4.1.89 becomes redundant.

However, the C-process in the case of गार्ग्य+छ+जस्, being oblivious to above-stated facts, proceeded with wrong derivational steps.

Instead of acknowledging its limitations, C-process tried to question the acumen of Maharshi Patañjali. For more clarification, see chapter no. 6, तद्धित section, example 3.

12. While deriving कालींमन्या, C-process indulged into rhetoric of questioning adhikāra and anuvṛtti process and suggested continuation of anuvṛtti of ह्रस्वः up to sūtra अरुर्द्विषदजन्तस्य मुम् (6.3.66). But, while commenting on Kaśikā's rationale, C-process grossly missed that already अजन्तस्य is read in the sūtra 6.3.66 thus making anuvṛtti of ह्रस्वः redundant. This is a manifestation of the failure and complexity of the C-process which proves that it has uncharitable disposition towards Indian seers.

Below is furnished padachheda (resolution of a

sentence into its constituent parts) of अरुर्द्विषदजन्तस्य मुम्

अरुर्द्विषदजन्तस्य(6.1), मुम् (1.1), [अच् अन्ते यस्य स अजन्तः, बहुव्रीहिः] [अरुश्च द्विषत् च अजन्तश्च अरुर्द्विषदजन्तं तस्य. समाहारो द्वन्द्वः]

13. C-process' prejudice against Indian seers is overtly displayed while expounding upon inference or meaning of sūtra यस्मात् प्रत्ययविधिस्तदादि प्रत्ययेऽङ्गम् (1.4.13). It has spent almost 3½ pages inferring the meaning of sūtra and critically evaluating the traditional interpretation. But all its efforts are in vain. His interpretation is quite misleading and farfetched, as already discussed in detail. On this sūtra, let us quote Maharshi Dayanand (1824-1893), a leading authority of Sanskrit Vyākaraṇa in modern times. In his Vedāṅgaprakāśa (Ākhyātika) and Aṣṭādhyāyī Bhāṣaya, he observes as follows:

"जिस धातु वा प्रातिपादिक से जिस प्रत्यय का विधान हो, वही प्रत्यय परे हो तो तदादि शब्द रूप, अर्थात् जिस से परे जो प्रत्यय करें उसी प्रत्यय के परे पूर्व रुप जो शब्द रुप है, सो अङ्ग सञ्ज्ञक हो और उस प्रत्यय का आदि अर्थात् प्रकृति और प्रत्यय के बीच में जो विकरण प्रत्यय है उसकी भी अङ्ग सञ्ज्ञा हो।"

This exposition of Maharishi Dayanand is clarified below:

राम+भ्यस्	राम is अङ्ग of भ्यस् because this pratyaya is preceded by prātipadika, राम.
चित्+लट्	चित् is अङ्ग of लट् because this pratyaya is preceded by चित् dhātu. (C-process failed to acknowledge the fact that लट् is कृदन्त् pratyaya)
चित्+तिप्	चित् is अङ्ग of तिप् because this pratyaya is preceded by चित् dhātu.
चित्+शप्+तिप्	चित् is अङ्ग of शप् pratyaya because it is

preceded by विकरण. शप् will be अङ्ग of तिप् pratyaya because it is preceded by तिप् and is placed between चित् prakṛti and तिप् pratyaya. चित्+शप् will together be treated as अङ्ग of तिप् pratyaya.

On closer analysis of the thesis, it is apparent that it indulged in futile exercise with an intention to disparage Indian seers' intellect. If we accept the concept of the C-process that in चित्+तिप्, चित् will not be अङ्ग of तिप् then we are faced with a new challenge and Pāṇinian process will be rendered unproductive. Below given example will prove the inefficiency of the C-process and the veracity of Ārṣa-vidhi:

In लुङ लकार derivation of भू dhātu, we arrive at this derivational equation:

अ+भू+सिच्+तिप्. (At this stage sūtra गातिस्थाघुपाभूभ्यः सिचः परस्मैपदेषु 2.4.77 initiates लुक् of सिच्)

अ+भू+तिप् (We arrive at this derivational step after लुक् of सिच्)

If we accept C-process then भू, due to स्थानिवत् of लुक्, will undergo operations induced by सिच्. This will, then, render sūtra भूसुवोस्तिङि (7.3.88) defunct which restricts गुण of 'भू' अङ्ग of 'तिप्' pratyaya.

From the above-stated fact, it is evident that Pāṇini's treatment of अङ्ग has been clearly exercised by traditional Ārṣa-vidhi, but the C-process misconceived the meaning of sūtra यस्मात् प्रत्ययविधिस्तदादि प्रत्ययेऽङ्गम् (1.4.13).

This misinterpretation has landed C-process into never ending dilemma and the same is evident in operation of sūtra अदिप्रभृतिभ्यः शपः (2.4.71) and जुहोत्यादिभ्यः

श्लुः (2.4.75).

The C-process, instead of giving preference to लुक and श्लु operation of शप्, first performed the operation with शप्, लुक् and श्लु. Thus, it is apparent that C-process requires operations related to pratyaya, which are to be replaced by लुक्, श्लु, आगम् or आदेश, etc., to be performed prior to any other operations. If we agree with this hypothesis, then it will even make the application of ल्यप् pratyaya more complex because here also, before replacement, operations related to त्त्वा pratyaya should be performed first.

14. Simplicity and consistency are the hallmark of the Ārṣa-vidhi, but the C-process lacking in this respect. Instead, it abruptly starts working on the derivational step ignoring fundamental Pāṇinian concepts. This flaw is demonstrated in the derivation of एध्+झ, the present third person plural form. We are anylizing this problem hereunder.

एध्	भूवादयो धातवः (1.3.1). This sūtra is अपवाद of प्रातिपादिक sūtra.
एध्+लट्	धातोः (3.1.91), प्रत्ययः (3.1.1) परश्च (3.1.2), वर्तमाने लट् (3.2.123)
एध्+ल्	At this step, two संज्ञा sūtras are applicable. यस्मात् प्रत्ययविधिस्तदादि प्रत्ययेऽङ्गम् (1.4.13) this sūtra makes एध् as अङ्ग of ल्, because ल् by virtue of sūtra कृदतिङ् (3.1.91) being अतिङ् is कृदन्त् pratyaya. Also by virtue of आर्धधातुकं शेषः (3.4.114) 'ल्' is आर्धधातुक pratyaya.
एध्+तिप्... महिङ्	For the sake of argument, we will follow C-process-derivation. It states that 1.4.13 and 3.4.114 do not block each other and

following the DOI operation of the C-process, we apply 3.4.114.

Sūtra 3.4.114 will entail operation of sūtra 3.4.77 and because of लस्य (3.4.77) sūtra तिप्तस्झिसिप्थस्थमिब्वस्मस्तातांझथाथांध्वमिड्वहिमहिङ्० (३।४।७८) is applicable.

Hence, we place तिप्तस्झिसिप्थस्थमिब्वस्मस्तातांझथाथांध्वमिड्वहिमहिङ्० to the right of एध्.

Here at this step, तिप्...महिङ् acquires two संज्ञा-

1. By virtue of sūtra तिङ्शित् सार्वधातुकम् (3.4.113) तिप्तस्झिसिप्थस्थमिब्वस्मस्तातांझथाथांध्वमिड्वहिमहिङ्० pratyaya will be treated as सार्वधातुक
2. By virtue of sūtra लः परस्मैपदम् (1.4.98), तिप्...महिङ् will be treated as परस्मैपद

As per the C-process this is a case of SOI and if we consider applicability, then both the sūtras are specific in nature.

Which sūtra is to be operated first? the C-process offers no clarification.

At this stage, C-process due to SOI and SOI-M is stuck and finds no way out. It simply starts operation with एध्+झ ignoring the fact that unless 18 pratyayas defined by तिप्...महिङ् are segregated into आत्मनेपद and परस्मैपद; first person, second person and third person; single, dual and plural forms, further derivation can't be carried on.

It is only after segregation of तिप्...महिङ्

pratyaya into आत्मनेपद, sūtra टित् आत्मनेपदानां टेरे (3.4.79) can be applied.

एध्+शप्+ तिप्...महिङ्

In example 9 of chapter 4, शस्+सिप्, example 28 (p. 152) and in other derivational examples, the C-process makes the following assumptions:

1. Sūtra कर्तरि शप् (3.1.68) does not block sūtra related to तिप्...महिङ्. (example-9)

It is to be noted that sūtra 3.1.68 is operative due to सार्वधातुक संज्ञा of तिप्...महिङ्.

2. Sūtra स्यतासि लृलुटोः (3.1.33) and sūtra टित आत्मनेपदानां टेरे (3.4.79) does not have any conflict. (example-28)

In addition to the above, at point no. 4.6 (pp. 166-169) the C-process expresses the same assumption.

These assumptions are irrational and as we move on further, derivation goes perilous.

However, if we follow thesis assumptions, then we will have the form placed in left-hand box and this lands C-process into catch-22 situation.

Because, when we apply शप् pratyaya between एध् and तिप्...महिङ् then we can never segregate तिप्...महिङ् into आत्मनेपद and परस्मैपद at all. This is because sūtra अनुदात्तङित आत्मनेपदम् (1. 3.12) is in ablative form and ablative form entails the absence of any pratyaya between prakṛti and pratyaya, i.e., there should not be any obstruction between एध् and तिप्...महिङ्.

From the above-stated facts, it is evident that the C-process selection of examples, and derivational steps are inconsistent and devoid of understanding of Pāṇinian mechanism. As such, C-process fails at every step of the derivation of verbal forms. For more clarification, see chapter no. 5, examples 7 and 8.

15. While performing an operation with धा+झि, third person plural form, C-process again committed a fundamental mistake as pointed out at point no. 13 of this chapter and in example 2 of the chapter no. 5. It has further made the following conjectures:

- धा dhātu will not be अङ्ग of झि.
- In the case of धा+शप्+झि instead of arriving at a form धा+झि after application of sūtra जुहोत्यादिभ्यः श्लुः (2.4.75), C-process arrives at form दा+श्लु+झि and then reduplicated धा dhātu, e.g. धा धा+श्लु+झि, by applying श्लौ (6.1.10).
- In footnote 11, page no. 114, the thesis treats vikaraṇa श्लु as pratyaya.
- In footnote 12, page no. 114, the thesis assumes the presence of pratyaya श्लु after धा dhātu.
- In धाधा+श्लु+झि equation, the thesis notifies that धा धा+श्लु cannot undergo any other operations which are not triggered by झि. Hence we can write धा धा+झि.

This conceptual fallacy has landed C-process' derivational process into a predicament situation and also rendered the following sūtras superfluous:

- अदर्शनं लोपः (1.1.59)

- प्रत्ययस्य लुक्श्लुलुपः (1.1.60)
- प्रत्ययलोपे प्रत्ययलक्षणम् (1.1.61)
- न लुमताङ्गस्य (1.1.62)

From the above sūtras, it is clear that "श्लु" renders invisibility (अदर्शन्) of pratyaya. Besides, in sūtra 6.1.10 श्लौ, श्लौ is in locative case (सप्तमी विभक्ति). The *"Paṭhana Pāṭhana kī Anubhūta Saralatama Vidhi"* describes three functions of locative case in Pāṇinian derivational process, as below:

"सप्तमी के तीन अर्थ होते हैं— **परे रहने पर, विषय में** या **निमित्त होने पर**। (इससे भिन्न ३।१।९२ से ३।४।११७ तक कहीं-कहीं सप्तमी का अर्थ **'उपपद'** भी होता है। उपपद सप्तमी के विषय में आगे समझायेंगे)"

It implies that locative case delineates three functions (i) placed after (ii) in the event of and (ii) being the cause.

In the present case, sūtra श्लौ (6.1.10) implies "in the event of" occurrence of श्लु and does not imply "placed after".

On analysis of the given situation and "श्लु" being the cause of invisibility, placement of 'श्लु' pratyaya by the C-process is in contravention of Pāṇinian principle. Further from narrations of the C-process, it can be deduced that it treats placement of 'श्लु' as स्थानिवत् and thus necessitate the application of अङ्ग operation due to शप्, श्लु pratyaya.

Surmises of the C-process pose certain problems which cannot be explained by it. Let us demonstrate it with the following examples:

- हु-(दानादनयोः, आदाने चेत्येके) dhātu (present case, third person, dual)

  As per C-process, the derivation is as under.

हु+शप्+तस् According to sūtra जुहोत्यादिभ्यः श्लुः (2.4.75) "शप्" pratyaya is replaced with श्लु and it is treated as pratyaya by C-process (see comment no 11, page no 114 of thesis).

At the next step, we receive the following equation:

हु+श्लु+तस् Since C-process agrees with postulation that हु will be अङ्ग of शप् pratyaya, therefore हु will also be treated as अङ्ग of श्लु pratyaya. श्लु being आदेश in place of शप् will be treated as स्थानिवत् (similar to the substituted). At this step, if we consider the interpretation of C-process, then हु dhātu will undergo two operations:

1. गुण operation by treating श्लु as सार्वधातुक which entails operation of sūtra सार्वधातुकार्धधातुकयोः (7.3.84).

2. Reduplication operation by virtue of sūtra श्लौ (6.1.10).

Since it is SOI operation and sūtra 7.3.84 and 6.1.10 do not block each other, then we will arrive at the following step:

हो हो+श्लु+तस् On reduplication and applying अभ्यास् sūtras, we will have following equation:

जुहो+श्लु+तस् An impossible equation and at the next step, by following C-process, we will have:

जुहो+तस् At this step, it is evident the C-process is whimsical in its approach and does not have any locus standi.

Note: - Kindly also refer to point no. 27 of this chapter.

16. While working with धा+झि, as noted at point no. 15, C-process derided Indian acumen by belittling the efficacy of the following three paribhāṣās:

P-54: - न चापवादविषये उत्सर्गोऽभिनिविशते।।

P-55: - पूर्वं ह्यपवादा अभिनिविशन्ते पश्चादुत्सर्गाः।।

P-56: - प्रकल्प्य चापवादविषयमुत्सर्गः प्रवर्त्तते।।

Maharshi Dayanand explains these three paribhāṣā as below:

“ये तीनों परिभाषायें उत्सर्गापवाद की व्यवस्था के लिये हैं। अपवाद विषय में उत्सर्ग की प्रवृत्ति नहीं होती। प्रथम अपवादों की और पश्चात् शेष विषय में उत्सर्गों की प्रवृत्ति होती है। अपवाद के विषय को छोड़ के अपने विषय में उत्सर्ग होते हैं।”

Aforementioned imply as under:

a). In case of simultaneous operation of अपवाद and उत्सर्ग (general) sūtras, अपवाद sūtras take precedence over general sūtras.

b). अपवाद sūtra will apply first followed by उत्सर्ग sūtra in rest of the matter.

c). उत्सर्ग sūtras do not deal with the issues of अपवाद sūtras. They will deal with issues which are not dealt with by अपवाद sūtras

However, C-process, on the strength of its derivational formula, tried to prove that the traditional method is random and absurd. But we have already shown at points no. 14 and 15 that the C-process is rampant with absurd analysis and whimsical methodology.

For more clarification, refer to the derivation of भि+झि, example 33, and धा+झि, chapter 6, आख्यातिक, example 2.

17. As we have specified above at points no. 14 and 15, fundamental mistakes have been committed by the C-process. Still, for the sake of argument, if we accept the thesis proposition, then we will encounter irrationality and randomness in the following derivational process:

Derivation of त्रैङ पालने ātmanepadi dhātu (present tense, second person, plural form, भ्वादि गण, by the Ārṣa-vidhi.

Derivation in Bhāṣā or Laukika Sanskrit usage	**Derivation in Vedic usage**
त्रै+शप्+ध्वम् We get त्राय्+अ+ध्वम् by sūtra एचोऽयवायावः (6.1.75)	त्रै+शप्+ध्वम् We get त्रै+ध्वम् by sūtra बहुलं छन्दसि (2.4.73) after लुक् of शप्, we get त्रा+ध्वम् + त्राध्वम् by sūtra आदेच उपदेशेऽशिति (6.1.44)

Now let us look at the derivation of त्रैङ् पालने dhātu by C-process in Vedic usage.

त्रै+शप्+ध्वम्
By sutra बहुलं छन्दसि (2.4.73) as per C-process, शप् will be replaced with लुक् and we will have
त्रै+लुक् +ध्वम्
Now since there is no

more application induced by ध्वम्, hence लुक् is elided and we will get त्रै+ध्वम् Applying आदेच उपदेशेऽशिति, we will get त्रा+ध्वम्. Thus, it is evident that C-process is irrational and random in its approach, as we have to resort to an extra step.

Here it may be argued that if we carry out this process with मुद् (हर्षे), आत्मनेपदि dhātu, in Vedic usage. Then on the application of लुक् and considering it to be स्थानिवत् (similar to the substituted one) we will have the following equations:

मुद्+शप्+ते

मुद्+लुक्+ते

मोद्+लुक्+ते (since लुक is स्थानिवत्, so will be treated as सार्वधातुक् and will entail गुण operation), and we will arrive at following form

मोद्+ते

But if we follow Ārṣa-vidhi, then we will have the following form:

मुद्+शप्+ते

मुद्+ते (After लुक्, i.e. अदर्शन् of शप् pratyaya. Since त, is अपित् and by sūtra सार्वधातुकं, अपित् will be ङित्व; hence गुण operation will not occur. This proves the complexity and irrationality of the C-process in applying लुक् and श्लु operations)

18. C-process bewilders us while working with

imperfect passive, third person singular form (लङ्, कर्मणि, प्रथमपुरुष, एकवचन) of वप् dhātu. If at the same place, the derivational equation of भू+तिप्, आशीर्लिङ् (benedictive), third person singular, page 141, example 19 is analyzed, then following conclusive statements can be arrived, based on C-process hypothesis:

a) वप् is not अङ्ग of त.
b) Since no vikaraṇa is added between भू and तिप् in आशीर्लिङ् forms, भू can be called a अङ्ग of तिप्.
c) C-process' respective interpretations of 1.4.13 and 6.4.1 ensure that the insertion of augment taught in the अङ्गाधिकार, takes place only after सम्प्रसारण, which is taught outside the अङ्गाधिकार.

If we assess the outcome of statements 'a' and 'b', then the perplexity of the thesis is mesmerizing. Big assumptions, but solutions are amazing and paradoxical. The statement at point 'a' and 'b' contradicts each other and point 'c' is a mere statement. The veracity of all these statements has already been tested in the foregoing discussions at points no. 13 to 16.

However, in the ensuing discussion, we will take up some more relevant points.

Sūtra 1.4.13 deals with pratyaya and all the pratyayas fall within the adhikara of sūtra प्रत्यय. (3.1.1) and परश्च (3.1.2). The adhikāra of these sūtras continue up to 5.4.160. Within the jurisdiction of this adhikāra lies the following two sūtras:

i. धातोरेकाचो हलादेः क्रियासमभिहारे यङ् (3.1.22), the anuvṛtti of धातोः from this sūtra goes up to 3.1.90 sūtra.

ii. धातोः (3.1.91) the adhikāra of this sūtra goes up to

sūtra 3.4.117.

If we review sūtra 3.1.22, then we will find that in its adhikāra, all the sūtras related to विकरण are instructed. While in the adhikāra of sūtra 3.1.91, lies कृत् and तिङ् pratyayas.

In light of the above observations, 1.4.13, with reference to 3.1.1, 3.1.2, 3.1.22 and 3.1.91, deals with pratyaya and does not distinguish between विकरण and other pratyayas. Hence sūtra 1.4.13 will treat यासुट्, सुट्, यक्, etc. equally. Because of this, C-process' conclusions are rampant with a random selection of steps and examples.

Still, on examination of statements at points 'a' and 'b', we can say that they are a rudimentary way of saying paribhāṣā-41 "विकरणेभ्यो नियमो बलीयान्."

Where as statement at point 'c' is also an elementary way of accepting paribhāṣā-106 "सम्प्रसारणं सम्प्रसारणाश्रयं च कार्यं बलीयो भवति."

Hence, it is pertinent to conclude that the C-process stands nowhere before the Ārṣa-vidhi.

For the derivation of वप्+त, refer to example 4, आख्यातिक section, chapter 6.

18. In the derivation of श्वि+त्त्वा, C-process contradicts itself as it deviates from its premise:

"My respective interpretations of 1.4.13 and 6.4.1 ensure that the addition of the augment, which is taught in the अङ्गाधिकार, takes place only after सम्प्रसारण, which is taught outside the अङ्गाधिकार." (refer to point no. 17c)

This premise is taught during derivation of वप्+त, example 4 of आख्यातिक् section, chapter 5, where also DOI operation exists. Contrary to this presumption, in the derivation of श्वि+त्त्वा, C-process instead of proceeding with सम्प्रसारण operation prefers operation with अङ्ग. This is a blatant violation of its own assertion and proof of the inconsistency of the methodology proposed in the thesis.

19. In the derivation of अतिक्रम्+त्त्वा C-process' complexity is exposed and proves the fact that self-proclaimed scholar of thesis lacks the understanding of the Pāṇinian derivational method. The following assumptions of the thesis corroborate our observations:

Commenting on sūtra समासेऽनञ्पूर्वे त्त्वो ल्यप् (7.2.37) and कुगतिप्रादयः (2.2.18) after derivational outcome, C-process states:

* It is important to point out the anomaly here. Pāṇini's rule 2.2.18 कुगतिप्रादयः teaches that the particle कु, items termed गति (including अति) and items belonging to the group headed by प्र (which also includes अति) combine with syntactically related padas to form तत्पुरुष compound. We know, thanks to 2.1.4 सह सुपा, that a compound composed of forms ending in सुप. Since the three forms क्रन्त्वा, क्रान्त्वा, क्रमित्वा (see example 4 of this section) end in सुप (which is replaced with लुक् by 2.4.82 अव्ययादाप्सुपः), अति can combine with any of these forms to construct a तत्पुरुष compound.

- To derive the correct form, we have to start the derivation by adding the verbal root क्रम् to अति which constitutes pūrvapada. To that, we add affix त्त्वा – अतिक्रम्+त्त्वा. This alone gives us the correct answer.

Here thesis missed the following points:

- While carrying out process of समास between अति+क्रम्, it accepts operation between सुबन्त pada and अति. By virtue of सह सुपा (2.1.4) and सुपो धातुप्रातिपदिकयोः (2.4.71), it performs समास operation. However, if we read sūtra उपपदमतिङ् (2.2.19) along with paribhāṣā sūtras quoted at point no. 9 then this premise of thesis is found fraught with never ending maze. Because if समास between गति/ कारक/ उपपद with कृदन्त is done after creation of सुबन्त, then in तद्धित operation अति and क्रम् pada will have separate प्रातिपादिक sañjñā.
- Due to this fallacious assumption, C-process will assign वृद्धि process at the latter pada and give the wrong form which is not in currency. This also goes against the Pāṇinian derivational process. For more clarification, kindly refer to the derivation of सांकूटिनम्, example-6, chapter 5.

In the process of demonstrating the precision of its method and trying to prove the fallibility of the traditional method, the thesis assumes as under:

❖ In the case of derivation of अति+क्रम्+त्त्वा, based on its presupposition, C-process attempts a review of the traditional method as follows:

a. Compound between अति+क्रन्त्वा, by 7.1.37 get अतिक्रन्त्य

b. Compound between अति+क्रान्त्वा, by 7.1.37 we get अतिक्रान्त्य

c. Compound between अति+क्रमित्वा, by 7.1.37 and

ह्रस्वस्य पिति कृति तुक् (6.1.69) we get अतिक्रमित्य.

C-process in support of its presupposition does not present any proof and unilaterally executes the incorrect derivational process in the name of the traditional approach.

However, in this process, thesis corroborates our conclusion about it, which has been referred to at points no. 15 and 16, that before the replacement of pratyaya by आदेश, श्लु, लुक्, ल्यप्, etc. the operation related to replaced pratyaya precede and then pratyayas to be replaced are affixed.

On the strength of the above-given facts, it is evident that the thesis, due to its prejudice towards Indian Ṛṣis' acumen, did not pay heed to their method. That is why, it could not comprehend the essence of paribhāṣā-48 "अन्तरङ्गानपि विधीन् बहिरङ्गो ल्यब् बाधते" which implies that ल्यप् pratyaya blocks operations induced by other pratyayas which it replaces.

20. In the derivation of रध्+णिच्, causative (प्रेरणार्थक), third-person singular, C-process committed serious blunders at following steps:

- When we get रध्+णिच् form, then, due to sūtra यस्मात् प्रत्ययविधिस्तदादि प्रत्ययेऽङ्गम् (1.4.13) and sūtra सनाद्यन्ता धातवः (3.1.32) two sañjñās become operational. रध् acquires अङ्ग sañjñā and रध्+णिच् acquires धातु sañjñā. Here neither DOI nor SOI operation can be claimed to perform systematically because रध् धातु acquires two sañjñās and both are specific in their nature. But if we go by C-process and somchow try to go by DOI operation, then derivation becomes haphazard and results in myriad complications of juxtaposing sūtras relating to सार्वधातुक, आत्मनेपद, परस्मैपद, एकवचन etc.

- The thesis' irrationality becomes more prominent if it is the case of चुर् dhātu of चुरादिगण. What will be the status of चुर्+णिच् and how will they react with तिप्, etc pratyaya in different tenses? It becomes a tickling point. If a concept similar to रध+णिच् is followed, then we are faced with more complexities, as we attempt derivation of causative (प्रेरणार्थक) form, we will get the following:

  चुर्+णिच्+णिच् here चुर् will be अङ्ग of first णिच्, चुर्+णिच् will be अङ्ग of second णिच्, whereas, simultaneously चुर्+णिच् and चुर्+णिच्+णिच् will acquire धातु sañjñā in addition to अङ्ग sañjñā.

- This methodology further gets complicated when we deal with सनन्त, etc. processes of the causative form of चुर dhātu. Because we will have the following equation:

  चुर्+णिच्+णिच्+सन् here too चुर् will be अङ्ग of first णिच्, चुर्+णिच् will be अङ्ग of second णिच् and चुर्+णिच्+णिच् will अङ्ग of सन्. Whereas, simultaneously, चुर्+णिच्, चुर्+णिच्+णिच् and चुर्+णिच्+णिच्+सन् will acquire धातु sañjñā in addition to अङ्ग sañjñā.

If we enter into the realm of प्रत्ययमाला then conceptual blunders of the C-process become obvious. Students are faced with juxtaposing various sūtras and then going through the maze of irrational DOI and SOI operations, which prove to be a nightmare.

On the contrary, Ārṣa-vidhi keeps the derivational process simple, cogent and easily comprehensible. The same can be witnessed in the derivation of the example of रध्+णिच्, (example 15, chapter 6).

21. In the derivation of ग्रह+तिप्, (लुङ्) aorist, third person, singular form, C-process is again caught on wrong foot. When अ+ग्रह+इ+स्+ई+त् equation is arrived, then by इट् ईटि (8.2.28) लोप of सिच् is done. Since this sūtra is read within the realm of पूर्वत्रासिद्धम् (8.2.1), therefore, it will be treated as असिद्ध (unknown) with respect to दीर्घ operation of इ+ई. Hence, we will not be able to do दीर्घ of इ+ई.

But C-process ignored this fact and proceeded with an impossible derivation and arrived at अग्रहीत्. How is दीर्घ operation achieved? The thesis does not offer any explanation. In this case vārttika "सिज्लोप एकादेशे सिद्धो वक्तव्यः" resolves this impasse and makes लोप of सिच् treating it as सिद्ध (known) and thus दीर्घ operation is accomplished.

Here, the adamancy of C-process, of not accepting the intelligence of Kātyāyana and Maharshi Patañjali, is exposed. This obstinate attitude has altogether, in many places, exposed the C-process to inevitable complications.

C-process on critical review is evidently selecting cases and examples that support its preconceived notion. The same is evident in the derivation process of गुपू dhātu, aorist, third-person, singular form. Here, it has eschewed derivational process ensuing as consequence of sūtras गुहूधूविच्छिपणिपनिभ्य आयः (3.1.28) and आयादय आर्धधातुके वा (3.1.31). If we follow C-process, then multiple sūtras will become applicable and this leads to a maze of illogical juxtaposing of sūtras.

Here, too C-process missed out at इट् ईटि (8.2.28), and झलो झलि (8.2.26) sūtra with respect to पूर्वत्रासिद्धम् (8.2.1) in case of लोप of सिच् pratyaya.

22. While deriving भिद्+त, aorist third person singular form, C-process, in case of लोप of सिच् pratyaya missed 8.2.1 sūtra with respect to sūtra झलो झलि (8.2.26).

23. Working with आशीर्लिङ्, benedictive, third-person singular form of भू+तिप्, C-process decries traditional astute observations. It exposed its vulnerability. The feebleness of the C-process is exposed in the following observations:

1. Since no विकरण vikaraṇa is added between भू and तिप् in आशीर्लिङ्, भू can be called a अङ्ग with respect to तिप्.

   It is pertinent to note that Maharshi Pāṇini never made any difference between विकरण and other pratyaya taught for dhātu. According to Pāṇini, स्य, तास्, शप्, श्यन्, यासुट्, सुट्, etc. under dhātu sañjñā have equal weight. This is the centre point of the weakness of the derivation of C-process. At point no. 17, we have already discussed this anomaly and the helplessness of C-process due to this concept. Since the Ārṣa-vidhi abides by Pāṇinian principle; hence its process does not get stuck into non-explainable situation.

2. Both sūtras संयोगान्तस्य लोपः (8.2.23) and स्कोः संयोगाद्योरन्ते च (8.2.29) are applicable. Both the sūtras are within the adhikāra of 8.2.1, but the thesis applied sūtra 8.2.29 instead of sūtra 8.2.23. It is amazing to note that it did not bother to offer a

reason for this failure, besides the logical reasoning offered in chapter 5 of the thesis which is full of contradictory assumptions.

The vārttika "संयोगादिलोपः संयोगान्तलोपे" offers solution to this. It says "जो त्रिपादी में संयोगादि सकार ककार का लोप होता है, वह संयोगान्त लोप करने के सिद्ध माना जावे।" That is, the application of पर sūtra (8.2.29) will be treated as सिद्ध (known) with respect to पूर्व sūtra (8.2.23).

Since, C-process, due to its obdurate attitude of disparaging Indian Maharshis, knowingly ignore this vārttika and hence offers a puny explanation. We will deliberate on this issue while discussing sūtra 8.2.1.

3. C-process failed to apply नित्य sūtra सुट् तिथोः (3.4.107) and did not offer any reason for this failure.

24. In the derivation of दिव्+त्त्वा, in निषेध option of sūtra उदितो वा (7.2.56), sūtra च्छ्वोः शूडनुनासिके च (6.4.19) becomes applicable. Sūtra 6.4.119 entails ऊठ् in place of व् of दिव् and we arrive at the following equation:

- दि ऊठ्+त्त्वा

At this step, being स्थानिवत् (similar to the substituted one) 'व्' will be considered to replace 'ऊठ्'. This situation will entail the operation of two sūtras (a) पुगन्तलघुपधस्य च 7.3.86, because of 'व' (b) इको यणचि 6.1.74 because of the interaction of इ of दि and ऊ of 'ऊठ्'.

Which of the two sūtras are to be applied? C-process failed to decide! Instead, it simply proceeded with sūtra 6.1.74, which shows its foolishness.

25. Whenever derivation becomes multifold and

involves a bit of complex application of sūtras, then the manifestation of inept deliberation of the C-process is visible. Derivation of कृ+सिप् is no exception to it, where it committed the following mistakes:

- ✓ At कुरू + हि step, due to sūtra हलि च (8.2.77) elongation (दीर्घ) of उ of कु is applicable.
- ✓ The application of sūtra 8.2.77 is restricted by sūtra न भकुर्छुराम् (8.2.79).

However, the thesis failed to acknowledge this fact and proceeded with the derivation process. The fundamental cause of this grave error is that C-process relied upon Laghu Siddhānta Kaumudi for the derivational step. Besides, its understanding of the Pāṇinian system is based upon the hybrid, occult, hypothetical process of neo-orientalist and occidentalist scholars. As this hybrid system failed to understand the Pāṇinian system, so is C-process. Here it is relevant to note the comment of Maharshi Dayanand. He observes:

"यहां भट्टोजिदीक्षित ने लिखा है कि (430, न भकुर्छुराम्) सूत्र यहां नहीं लगता क्योंकि वहां कुर् कहने से कृञ् धातु का ग्रहण होता है। इससे 'कूर्यात' प्रयोग होता है सो संदिग्ध है क्योंकि जो (लक्षणप्रतिपदोक्तयो:०) इस परिभाषा का आश्रय करें तब कृञ् धातु का ही न हो क्योंकि कृञ् का कुर् लाक्षणिक और कुर् धातु प्रतिपदोक्त है इसलिये इस परिभाषा का आश्रय न करें तो भी लाक्षणिक और प्रतिपदोक्त दोनों का ग्रहण होवे। फिर ऐसी परिभाषा कौन है कि जिससे लाक्षणिक कृञ् का ग्रहण हो जावे और प्रतिपदोक्त कुर् का न हो।"

In a nutshell, this statement of Maharshi Dayanand points out the mistake of Siddhānta Kaumudī and clarifies that sūtra 8.2.79 is applicable for both कुर् and कृ dhātus.

26. The C-process though is irrationally overcritical of Mahābhāṣya, yet its own methodology is another hoax. If we critically analyse the derivation of भू+त, passive aorist third-person singular (कर्मणि, लुङ्), then the mess created by C-process is exposed. Hereunder, we are indicating major mistakes committed by C-process:

भू+सिच्+त	This derivational step is arrived at by affixing of लुङ् pratyaya after भू dhātu. Subsequently, after categorization of आत्मनेपद्, etc. we arrive at भू+त and thereafter by sūtra च्लि लुङि (3.1.43) and च्लेः सिच् (3.144) we arrive at भू+सिच्+त form. At this step, if we agree with the C-process, then भू+सिच् will be अङ्ग of त and this should entail the operation of sūtra लुङ्लङ्लृङ्क्ष्वडुदात्तः (6.4.71), but thesis skipped this step and proceeded further without offering any tangible reason for this omission.

In the case of the example 14 of भू+तिप्, aorist third-person singular at page no. 135, same procedural mistake has been committed.

27. Following comment made by the student during the derivation of भि+झि, the present third-person plural, depicts the failure of DOI/SOI principle.

> "Note that the optional rule 6.4.115 भियोऽन्तरस्याम्, although applicable, does not end up applying in this derivation. So even if we had not implemented the optional rule 6.4.115, we would still have got the same form, i.e. बिभ्यति"

From the above observation and on analysis of the derivational approach adopted, it is clear that C-process could not understand the role of अभ्यस्त sañjñā sūtra. It is relevant to note that अभ्यस्त sañjñā sūtra precedes other sūtras and thus entails the operation of अदभ्यस्तात् (7.1.4) sūtra and this sūtra blocks the operation of sūtra 6.4.115. However, C-process, throughout its derivational method, never referred to this fact.

Besides it, the above-referred comment is the proof of a rudimentary understanding of the Pāṇinian system by C-process. It further proves that it is just an exercise of juxtaposing different sūtras to arrive at the final form without caring for the Pāṇinian derivational system.

28. If a person becomes so much engrossed with his own self and starts blowing his own trumpet, then he starts discarding the established norms without any reason. The same attitude is flaunted while dealing with the derivation of व्यध्+त्त्वा. In exhibiting the efficacy of SOI operation, the thesis exposed the redundancy and weakness of the C-process. It unnecessarily over stretched sūtra 6.1.16 ग्रहिज्यावयिव्यधिवष्टिविचतिवृश्चतिपृच्छतिभृतिभृज्जतीनां ङिति च, though sūtra न सम्प्रसारणे सम्प्रसारणम् (6.1.36) which is पर sūtra, already defines the applicability of 6.1.16.

29. In chapter five of the thesis, C-process has contended the interpretation of असिद्धवत् and असिद्धम् by Indian Ṛṣis.

With regard to the contention of C-process concerning the meaning of असिद्धवत् and असिद्धम्, Paribhāṣā-102, from पारिभाषिक of Maharshi Dayanand, suitably reply to the unnecessary dispute created by C-process:

"पर्यायशब्दानां लाघवगौरवचर्चा नाद्रियते"

Maharshi Dayanand defines above Paribhāṣā as "लाघव गौरव का विचार सर्वत्र रहता है जहाँ तक हो थोड़ा वचन पढ़के बहुत अर्थ निकालना, परन्तु पर्याय शब्दों में थोड़े बहुत होने का विचार नहीं करते कि जहां थोड़े वचन से काम चल सकता है, तो उसका पर्याय अधिक अक्षर का शब्द न पढ़ना।

जैसे- अन्यतरस्याम्, विभाषा वा उभयथा इत्यादि एकार्थ शब्दों को पढ़ दिया, यह नियम नहीं कि इतना अधिक क्यों पढ़ा, इत्यादि।"

"The idea of brevity is everywhere, as far as possible, deriving a lot of meaning by reading a few words, but do not think of applying the idea of brevity in the case of synonyms, that where the purpose is served with brevity, then do not use lengthy synonym.

Like - Anyatarasyām, Vibhāṣā or Ubhayathā, etc. are words read conveying same meaning. There is no rule of using brief or lenghty words."

Now, in the light of above explanation it is clear that argument raised by C-process is irrelevant and goes against very nature of Pāṇinian system.

30. It becomes clear from the assumptions made by C-process in Appendix A, Appendix B and Appendix C, that it is in a state of dire confusion and is bereft of basic knowledge of the Pāṇinian derivational process. Some of the major assumptions made by the C-process are as follows:

There is no evidence in the words of sūtra आदेः परस्य (1.1.53) or elsewhere to suggest that the presence of an ablative form in an operational rule constitutes a necessary condition for its application.

Sūtra अलोऽन्त्यस्य (1.1.51) and sūtra ङिच्च (1.1.52) are

taught for left hand side substitution (LHS). Sūtra आदेः परस्य (1.1.53) is taught for right hand side (RHS) and sūtra अनेकाल्शित् सर्वस्य (1.1.54) is taught for both RHS and LHS. The sūtra तस्मिन्निति निर्दिष्टे पूर्वस्य (1.1.65) merely indicates the left-hand side and तस्मादित्युत्तरस्य (1.1.66) indicates right hand side. It does not indicate "in place of left-hand side or right-hand side" for 1.165 and 1.1.66, respectively.

In chapters no. 7 and 8, we have debunked the understanding of the C-process and have also proved that all these sūtras, viz. 1.1.54, 1.1.52, 1.1.53, 1.1.54, 1.1.65 and 1.1.66 are to be read in with respect to each other.

31. In Appendix B, C-process has disapproved interpretation of Ārṣa-vidhi for the following sūtras:

आद्यन्तौ टकितौ (1.1.45): "षष्ठी निर्दिष्ट को टित् तथा कित् आगम् कहा गया है, वह क्रम से उसका आदि और अन्त अवयव हो, षष्ठी स्थानेयोगा (1.1.48) का पूर्व अपवाद है।" (Prathmāvṛtti, Pandit Brahmdutt Jigyasu)

दीर्घात् पदान्ताद् वा (6.1.73): "जो अपदान्त अर्थात् एकपद में दीर्घ से परे छकार हो, तो उसको तुक का आगम होता है। जो पदान्त दीर्घ से परे छकारादि उत्तरपद हो, तो उसको तुक का आगम विकल्प करके होता है।" (Maharshi Dayanand, Vedāṅga Prakash-Sandhi Viṣaya)

C-process while disapproving Ārṣa-vidhi's interpretation commented as follows:

> I don't think that we should take liberty to read षष्ठी निर्दिष्ट "taught in the genitive", into sūtra 1.1.45. It simply means items marked with ट् and items marked with क् should be attached to the beginning and end respectively.
>
> I don't think that there is any competition between 1.1.65 and 1.1.67. I think both 1.1.65 and 1.166 are required to interpret 6.1.76.

To support its mysterious blunder, cover up gross error and obscure scientific approach of Indian seers, it has quoted example of कुटिच्छाया.

Though we have dealt with this issue in chapters no. 7 and 8, still it is obligatory on our part to clarify the unwarranted confusion created by C-process.

In chapter six, prathama pāda, from sūtra no 6.1.69 to sūtra 6.1.73 तुक आगम is taught. All the sūtras are given below: -

ह्रस्वस्य पिति कृति तुक (6.1.69), [Adhikara of ह्रस्वस्य goes up to 6.1.71, and of तुक up to 6.1.73]

छे च (6.1.71), [Adhikara of छे goes up to 6.1.73]

आङ् माङोश्च (6.1.72)

दीर्घात् पदान्ताद् वा (6.1.73)

In sūtra 6.1.72 आङ् and माङ् (उपसर्ग) are in the genitive case and they have long vowel (आ). Besides, both are पद by virtue of अव्यय sañjñā.

Sūtra 6.1.73 follows sūtra 6.1.72 and teach अपदान्त and पदान्त दीर्घ (long vowels). They are other than 'आ' taught in sūtra 6.1.72. Hence it is अपवाद of sūtra 6.1.72 and has to be read with reference to this sūtra. Due to this reason, तुक has to be mandatorily augmented on left hand side long vowel.

If sūtra 6.1.73 is not read with reference to sūtra 6.1.72, than it defeats the very purpose of Pāṇini of placing sūtra 6.1.73 after 6.172.

Besides, it is relevant to note that Maharshi Patañjali has quoted the following vārttika at sūtra 6.1.73 which further corroborates Ārṣa-vidhi.

Vārttika: "विश्वजनादीनां छन्दस्युपसंख्यानम्", Maharshi Dayanand describes it as "विश्वजन आदि शब्दों से परे छकार को विकल्प करके तुक् का आगम होता है।"

It implies that तुक is optionally augmented when छ is followed by विश्वजन, etc. This vārttika is an exception to sūtra 6.1.71.

Still, if the premise of C-process is accepted, then it can be argued why not sūtras from 6.1.69 to 6.1.72 are read in ablative (पञ्चमी) case? Besides, the C-process' argument will be faced with another problem of application of मित् pratyaya, for example, रुधादिभ्यः श्नम् (3.1.78) where सार्वधातुके is in the locative case and रुधादिभ्यः is in ablative case.

32. In Appendix A, while deriving लिखितात्, C-process has rejected Kātyāyana's vārttika, which states that the ङ् of तातङ् is सावकाश 'operated elsewhere' [we can infer that] there is a vipratieṣedha 'conflict' (between 1.1.54 *anekālsit sarvasya* and 1.1.52 ङिच्च) [and thus, the para-rule, which teaches [sarvādeśa], [wins], on following grounds: -

* We know that, in Pāṇini's grammar, if a certain item is marked with ङ्, then it automatically possesses all the properties associated with ङ-marking, unless Pāṇini has said something to the opposite effect. One cannot arbitrarily choose which function of ङ् is relevant to a particular rule and which function is not. Thus, Kātyāyana's explanation is not acceptable.'

The above statement of C-process is conclusive evidence that it has a myopic view of Pāṇinian system. He has relied on tertiary sources, which are based on the work of neo-orientalist and occidentalist Sanskrit grammarians who are devoid of in-depth knowledge of Ārṣa-vidhi.

Maharshi Dayanand, based on Mahābhāṣya's exposition, in Vedāṅga Prakāśa provides solution to this question, which is furnished below:

(प्रश्न) तातङ् आदेश अन्त्य अल् के स्थान में प्राप्त है, सो क्यों नहीं होता?

(उत्तर)- भा- एवं तर्ह्येतदेव ज्ञापयति, न तातङन्त्यस्य स्थाने भवतीति-यदेतं ङितं करोति। इतरथा हि लोट एरुप्रकरण एव ब्रूयात् तिह्योस्तादाशिष्यन्यतरस्यामिति ।। महा. 1.1.52 ।।

यह इसी सूत्र पर महाभाष्यकार ने समाधान किया है कि- जिस कारण तातङ् आदेश ङित् किया है, इसी से आचार्य की शैली स्पष्ट विदित होती है कि यह अन्त्य अल् स्थान में नही होता। जो अन्त्य अल् के स्थान में करना होता तो तृतीयाऽध्याय के चतुर्थपाद में "लोटो लङ्वत्"; "एरुः" इन सूत्रों के आगे 'तात्' आदेश कहते, इस में लाघव भी बहुत आता था।

जो लोट् लकार का 'ति' और 'हि' का होकर उसको तात् आदेश विकल्प करके होवे, ऐसा कहने से अन्त्य अल् इकार के स्थान मे हो ही जाता, फिर अङ्गात्र के अधिक पढ़ने और सप्तमाध्याय के प्रथमपाद में तातङ् आदेश कहने से ठीक जाना जाता है कि तातङ् आदेश में ङित् करण गुण वृद्धि प्रतिषेध आदि के लिये हैं, इस कारण अन्त्य अल् के स्थान में नहीं होता।।

Above illustration of Maharshi Dayanand implies following salient points: -

- If तातङ् was to replace final sound then तात् could have been read after "लोटो लङ्वत्" and "एरुः". This would have accorded brevity to the Pāninian derivation.
- Besides, if it has also been said that तात् is optionally applicable to 'ति' and 'हि', then it would have become applicable to the final sound.

- Marking तात् by ङ् and reading it in the seventh chapter, prathama adhyāya explicitly indicates that ङ् of तातङ् is only to restrict गुण and वृद्धि operation.

The above interpretation of Maharshi Dayanand establishes the supremacy of Ārṣa-vidhi which directly emanates from Indian Ṛṣis. It also proves that C-process has failed at every step and is devoid of Pāṇinian derivational method. Instead of understanding Pāṇini, it has relied on Kaumudī process, which is to date a nemesis for Sanskrit Grammarians.

33. C-process has needlessly raised doubt about the nominal case of सन्यङोः (6.1.9). In Ārṣa-vidhi tradition, it was nowhere treated as a locative (सप्तमी) case. It has always been treated as genitive (षष्ठी) case. Had Pāṇini wanted to treat it as locative case, he would have read it as one sūtra along with लिटि धातोरनभ्यासस्य (6.1.8), श्लौ (7.1.10) and चङि (7.1.11) which are in locative case. Therefore, the arrangement of sūtra is proof of genitive case of sūtra 6.1.9.

Besides, sūtra सनाद्यन्ताधातवः (3.1.32) also indicates that sūtra सन्यङोः has to be in genitive case so that derivational method of Pāṇini remains cogent.

Chapter - 5

The Ārṣa-vidhi

In this chapter, we will deal with the mechanism of the Ārṣa-vidhi so that readers may be able to appreciate the simplicity and understand the scientific approach of this derivational method.

In addition to Paribhāṣās already discussed in chapters 2 and 3, we are here delving into a few more important Paribhāṣās.

Before proceeding to derivational examples, readers should read the following statements of Maharshi Dayanand on Paribhāṣā 11 and 67:

P-11: - अर्थवत आगमस्तद्गुणीभूतोऽर्थवद् ग्रहणेन गृहयते।।

arthavata āgamastadguṇībhūto'rthavad grahaṇena gṛhayate । ।

जो नागेश और भट्टोजिदीक्षित और नवीन लोग इस परिभाषा को (यदागमास्तद् गुणीभूतास्तद् ग्रहणेन गृह्यन्ते) इस प्रकार की लिखते मानते और व्याख्यान भी करते हैं, सो महाभाष्य से विरुद्ध है। महाभाष्य में यह परिभाषा ऐसी कहीं नहीं लिखी। इसलिये इन लोगों का प्रमाद है।

[Meaning] Nagesh and Bhattoji Dixit, etc. neo-grammarians write, believe and teach the above paribhāṣā (metarule) like *yadāgamastad guṇībhūtāstad grahaṇena gṛhyante*. It is against the Mahābhāṣya. This definition is not written anywhere in the Mahābhāṣya. This is the errot of these people.

P-67: - साम्प्रतिकाऽभावे भूतपूर्वगतिः।।

sāmpratikā'bhāve bhūtapūrvagatiḥ

यहां भूतपूर्वगति परिभाषा के मानने से कार्य भी चल जाता, तथा अन्यत्र भी सब काम चलता है, 'कुमार्यै ब्राह्मणाय' इत्यादि प्रयोग सिद्धि के लिये नदी संज्ञा में (प्रथमलिङ्गग्रहणञ्च) इस वार्तिक का भी कुछ प्रयोजन नहीं रहा। क्योंकि इस परिभाषा के होने से सब काम निकल जाते हैं। **वार्तिक एकदेशी और परिभाषा सर्वदेशी है।।**

[Meaning] Here and elsewhere, purpose can be served by following the above metarule. For the proof of of '*kumāryai brāhmaṇāya*' etc. in nadi sañjñā, vārttika- '*prathamliṅgagrahaṇañcha*' also not required. Because this metarule serves all purposes. Application of vārttika is limited, but application of metarule is universal.

In nutshell, Maharshi Dayanand has indicated two important and relevant points:

1. Neo-Indian Sanskrit grammarians, namely Bhaṭṭoji Dixit and Nagesh, etc. have stated and interpreted many paribhāṣās which are not supported by Patañjali's Mahābhāṣya.

2. Application of paribhāśās is universal, whereas application of vārttikas is limited and confined to a particular topic or subject.

Ārṣa-vidhi: - Some important Paribhāṣās

P: -38) पूर्वपरनित्यान्तरङ्गाऽपवादानामुत्तरोत्तरं बलीयः।।

पूर्व से पर, पर से नित्य, नित्य से अन्तरङ्ग, और अन्तरङ्ग से अपवाद ये सब पूर्व से उत्तर उत्तर बलवान होते हैं।

This paribhāṣā implies that पर sūtra is stronger with respect to पूर्व sūtra, नित्य sūtra is stronger with respect to पर sūtra, अन्तरङ्ग sūtra is stronger with respect to नित्य sūtra and अपवाद sūtra is stronger with respect to अन्तरङ्ग sūtra. These sūtras are stronger with respect to each other in their respective order. Thus, it is apparent that अपवाद

sūtra is the strongest of all.

Let us understand this by the following examples: -

1. अत्रेरपत्यम् - आत्रेयः

"अत्रि" being a name of a Ṛṣi, is the subject of तस्यापत्यम्. Thus sūtra ऋष्यन्धकवृष्णिकुरुभ्यश्च (४।१।११४) is applicable here. As such, अण् pratyaya is to be affixed after अत्रि.

However, अत्रि has two vowels and ends with vowel 'इ'. Therefore, by virtue of sūtra इतश्चानिञः (4.1.122) ढक् pratyaya also becomes applicable.

Thus, sūtras 4.1.114 and 4.1.122 are applicable here.

Since 4.1.122 is पर sūtra, it will block pūrva sūtra 4.1.114, so ढक् pratyaya will be applied and we arrive at the following:

अत्रि+ङस्+ढक्....अत्रि+ढक्....(किति च, 7.2.118) (यस्येति च...)

आत्र्+ढक्..(आयनेयीनीयियः फढखछघां प्रत्ययादीनाम् 7.1.2)...

आत्रेय+सु.....आत्रेयः

2. भू+अ (णल्) (Kindly refer to examples 7, 8 and 9 of this chapter)

At this stage following sūtras are applicable:

लिटि धातोरनभ्यासस्य (6.1.8)

liṭi dhātoranabhyāsasya (6.1.8)

इको यणचि (6.1.74)

iko yaṇachi (6.1.74)

अचि श्नुधातुभ्रुवां य्वोरियङुवङौ (6.4.77)

achi śnudhātubhruvāṁ yvoriyaṅvaṅau (6.4.77)

सार्वधातुकार्धधातुकयोः (7.3.84)

sārvadhātukārdhadhātukayoḥ (7.3.84)

अचो ञ्णिति (7.3.115)

acho ñṇiti (7.3.115)

भुवो वुग् लुङ् लिटोः (6.4.88)

bhuvo vug luṅ liṭoḥ (6.4.88)

Here 6.1.8 being नित्य sūtra blocks the operation of पर sūtra 6.1.74.

6.4.77 being अन्तरङ्ग sūtra, blocks the operation of sūtra 6.1.8.

7.3.84 being अपवाद of sūtra 6.4.77, blocks the operation of 6.4.77.

7.3.115 beins अपवाद of sūtra 7.3.84, blocks the operation of 7.3.84.

6.4.88 being अपवाद of sūtra 7.3.84 and 7.3.115, blocks the operations of 7.3.84 and 7.3.115.

As such, we are left with sūtra 6.1.8, which is नित्य and sūtra 6.4.88. So, sūtra 6.4.88, being पर sūtra with respect to 6.1.8 will be applied first followed by 6.1.8 and we get the following at the next step:

भू वुक् अ

Paribhāṣā: 43 & 44) असिद्धं बहिरङ्गमन्तरङ्गे ।। (43)

asiddhaṁ bahiraṅgamantaraṅge (43)

असिद्धं बहिरङ्लक्षणमन्तरङ्गलक्षणे ।। (44)

asiddhaṁ bahiraṅlakṣaṇamantaraṅgalakṣaṇe (44)

Maharishi Dayanand explains these two paribhāṣās as under:

"बहिरङ्ग उसको कहते हैं कि प्रकृति, प्रत्यय, वर्ण और पद के समुदाय में जिस कार्य के उपकारी अवयव दूसरे कार्य की अपेक्षा से दूर वा अधिक हों। और 'अन्तरङ्ग' वह कहाता है कि प्रकृति आदि निमित्तों के समुदाय से जिस कार्य के उपकारी अवयव दूसरे कार्य की अपेक्षा में समीप वा न्यून हों। तथा जो बहुत निमित्त और व्याख्यान की अपेक्षा रक्खे वह बहिरङ्ग तथा थोड़े निमित्त और अपेक्षा रखें वह अन्तरङ्ग कहाता है।"

It implies that when in the interacting groups of प्रकृति, प्रत्यय, वर्ण and पद, when a cause of action lies outside or involves more components as compared to others, then it is termed as बहिरङ्ग. When the cause of action lies inside, or within, or involves fewer components as compared to others, it is called अन्तरङ्ग. Besides, that which requires many bases and expositions is also termed as बहिरङ्ग, whereas, that which requires fewer bases and expositions is called अन्तरङ्ग.

On the basis of the above definition, Āchārya Pradyuman has further explained it as follows:

एकाश्रितमन्तरङ्गम, बह्वाश्रितं बहिरङ्गम्।

ēkāśritamantaraṅgama, bahvāśritaṁ bahiraṅgam ।

Operation based upon one item is antaraṅga and that which is based upon many is bahiraṅga.

प्रकृत्याश्रितमन्तरङ्गम्, प्रत्ययाश्रितं बहिरङ्गम्।

prakṛtyāśritamantaraṅgam,pratyayāśritaṁ bahiraṅgam ।

Operation based upon prakṛti is antaraṅga and that which is based upon pratyaya is bahiraṅga.

पूर्वोपस्थितिकमन्तरङ्गम्, परोपस्थितिकं बहिरङ्गम्।

pūrvopasthitikamantaraṅgam, paropasthitikaṁ

bahiraṅgam ।

Operation based upon 'pūrva' is antaraṅga and that which is based upon 'para' is bahiraṅga.

पूर्वोपस्थितनिमित्तकमन्तरङ्गम्, परोपस्थितनिमित्तकं बहिरङ्गम् ।

pūrvopasthitanimittakamantaraṅgam, paropasthita-nimittakaṁ bahiraṅgam

Operation that which has 'pūrva' as a cause of action or place is antaraṅga, whereas that which has 'para' as the cause or place of action is bahiraṅga.

Let us understand this by the following examples:

1. स्योनः

सिवु	Following sūtras are applicable (सिवेष्टेर्यु च) - उणादि-39; च्छ्वोः शूडनुनासिको च (6.4.19)
सि ऊ +न	Now considering स्थानिवत् (similar to the substituted one) condition of 'व' we have लघूपधगुण of इ by sūtra पुगन्तलघुपधस्य च (7.3.84) and यण by sūtra इको यणचि (6.1.74). The cause of यण (इ+ऊ) lies within as compared to cause of गुण (न) which lies outside. So, यण is अन्तरङ्ग and गुण is बहिरङ्ग. Hence, we arrive the following at the next step:
स्यू+न	At this step applying sūtra पुगन्तलघुपधस्य च (7.3.84), we get the following at the next step
स्योन+सु	

2. दुद्यूषति

दिव्+सन्	By sūtra सनीवन्तर्धभ्रस्जदम्भुश्रिस्वृयूर्णुभरज्ञ-पिसनाम् (7.2.49), दिव् dhātu इव्-ending, इट् is applied optionally. If we go by निषेध option, sūtra हलन्ताच्च (1.2.10) treat सन् pratyaya as कितवत्. Subsequently, sūtra च्छ्वोः शूडनुनासिको च (6.4.19) is applied and we have get the following at the next step:
दि ऊठ्+सन्	Since सन् is कितवत्, गुण operation is blocked. At this step following sūtras are applicable. 1. इको यणचि (6.1.74) which is अन्तरङ्ग and initiate यण सन्धि. 2. सन्यङोः (6.1.9) which is नित्य and initiate reduplication. 6.1.74 being अन्तरङ्ग, will apply first.
द्यू+सन्	Now by नित्य sūtra 6.1.9, reduplication occurs and by अभ्यास् process, we have the following at the next step:
दुद्यू+सन्+तिप्	Sūtra सनाद्यन्ता धातवः (3.1.22) assigns dhātu sañjñā and entails application of तिबादि pratyayas.

3. द्युकामः (दिवि कामो यस्य सः, One who desires Dyauloka)

दिव् ङि काम सु	By sūtra अनेकमन्यपदार्थे (2.2.24), कृत्तद्धित समासाश्च (1.2.46), सुपधातुप्रातिपदिकयोः (2.4.71), we have the following at the

next step:

दिव्+काम् — By sūtra दिव् उत् (6.1.127) and अलोऽन्तस्य (1.1.51), व् is replaced with उ.

दि उ+काम् — At this step, due to स्थानिवत्, लोपो व्योर्वलि (6.1.64) sūtra entails लोप of उ. But sūtra अनल्विधौ blocks लोप operation. Under the circumstances, इको यणचि (6.1.74) initiates यण सन्धि and we have the following at the next step:

द्युकाम+सु — At this step, sūtra कृत्तद्धित समासाश्च (1.2.46) makes prātipadika sañjā and sūtra अत इञ् (4.1.95) teaches the addition इञ् (इ) suffix, so we get the following at the next step:

द्युकाम+इ — At this step, sūtra यस्येति च (6.4.148) and तद्धितेष्वचामादेः (7.2.117) are applicable. Both the sūtras are नित्य but sūtra 6.4.148 is अन्तरङ्ग while sūtra 7.2.117 is बहिरङ्ग. Hence sūtra 6.4.148 is applied first followed by 7.2.117 and we arrive at the following step:

द्यौकाम्+इ

4. व्येञ्+अनियर्

व्यै+अनीय् — Sūtra आदेच उपदेशेऽशिति (6.144) being अन्तरङ्ग will precede sūtra एचोऽयवायावः (6.1.75) and we arrive at the next step

व्या+अनीय्

Note: Here it is pertinent to note that anuvṛtti of धातोः from sūtra 6.1.8 comes by मण्डूकप्लुति न्याय to sūtra 6.1.44.

5. आटिटत् (उसने भ्रमण किया)

अट्	भूवादयो धातवः (3.1.1), हेतुमति च (3.1.26)
अट् णिट्	अत उपधायाः (72.116), वृद्धिरादैच (1.1.1)
आट् इ	सनाद्यन्ता धातवः (3.1.32), धातोः (3.1.91), लुङ् (3.2.110), प्रत्ययः (3.1.1), परश्च (3.1.2)
आट् इ लङ्	Here after तिबादि operations, we get the following
आट् इ ति	च्लि लुङि (3.1.43), णिश्रिद्रुस्रुभया कर्तरि चङ् (3.1.48)
आट् इ अ(चङ्) ति	इतश्च (3.4.100)
आट् इ अ त्	At this step, by sūtra णेरनिटि (6.4.51), इ of णिच् is elided. But, here, by sūtra णौ चङ्युपधाया ह्स्वः (7.4.1), penultimate vowel is shortened. Since the cause of action for sūtra 7.4.1 is dependent on the presence of णिच्+चङ्, whereas लोप of इ of णिच् is dependent on चङ्. Hence, sūtra 7.4.1 is बहिरङ्ग and लोप of णिच् which is नित्य and अन्तरङ्ग takes place. Hence, we arrive at the next step:
आट् अ त्	By चङि (6.1.11), which is नित्य sūtra, reduplication of आट् is applicable. But, since णिच् is absent here; so sūtra 7.4.1 and 6.1.11 are not applicable. In this situation, by sūtra द्विर्वचनेऽचि, pratyaya इ (णिच्) is deemed to be

present.

In both operations, चङ् is the cause of action. But, if we closely analyse the case of reduplication, only चङ् is involved, whereas in the application of sūtra 7.4.1 णिच्+चङ् is involved.

Besides, it is to be noted that चङ् pratyaya is obtained due to the presence of णिच्. Hence reduplication process cannot be treated as अन्तरङ्ग with respect to sūtra 7.4.1.

The reduplication process is नित्य, but due to the insertion of णिच् which is बहिरङ्ग with respect to sūtra 7.4.1, the shortening of a vowel is to be performed first.

अ ट (इ) अ त् — Now since we have इ आदेश by sūtra इतश्च 3.4.100, द्विर्वचनेऽचि teaches us reduplication of टि and we arrive at the next step

अ टि ट् अ त् — After application of sūtra आडजादीनाम (6.4.72), etc. we arrive at the next step

आट् अ टि ट् अ त्

With reference to the above, it is pertinent to quote Maharshi Dayanand's interpretation of Mahābhāṣya 7.4.1.

Maharshi Dayanand while discussing derivation of आटिटत् says "आटिटत् यहां उपधा को ह्रस्व बहिरङ्ग है परन्तु ओण् धातु में ऋदितकरणसामर्थ्य मान द्वित्व से पहिले ही ह्रस्व हो जाता है।"

It implies that in āṭiṭat, the action of shortening of

penultimate is bahiraṅga, but so far as oṇa dhātu is concerned, in the case of elision of ṛt, the action of shortening takes place prior to reduplication.

Let us see derivation of causative form of चुर् dhātu of चुरादि गण, in लुङ् लकार. (चोरयन्तं प्रेरयति= चोरयति)

6. अचुचुरत्

अ+चोर्+इ (णिच्)+इ (णिच्)+अ (चङ्)+त्

इस अवस्था में णिच् के परे प्रथम णिच् का लोप होता है। उपधाह्रस्वत्व करते समय पूर्व णिच् स्थानिवत् हो जाता है। इसलिये जिस णिच् का व्यवधान है। जो णिच्(प्रथम) ह्रस्वभावी अङ्ग से परे है उससे परे चङ् नहीं, द्वितीय णिच् का व्यवाधान है, अतः यहां ह्रस्वत्व की प्राप्ति नहीं होती। ऐसी अवस्था में 'णेर्णिच्युपसंख्यानम्'(महाभाष्य 7.4.1) इस वार्तिक से या 'ण्याकृतिनिर्देशात् सिद्धम्' (महा 7.4.1) इस आकृतिग्रहण से ह्रस्वत्व होता है।

[Meaning] In this state, the first ṇich followed by another ṇich is omitted. While shortening penultimate vowel, the former ṇich becomes similar to the substituted one. That's why, the ṇich which is going to intervene, the one (first ṇich) which is followed by aṅga, to be shortened, having no chaṅ following it, where there is intervention of second ṇich; hence shortening action does not take place. In such a situation, by vārttika '*ṇerṇichyupasaṅkhyānam*' (Mahābhāṣya 7.4.1) or by '*nyākṛti nirdeśāt siddham*' (Māhābhāṣya 7.4.1) operation of shortening takes place.

Similarly, Maharshi Dayanand, with respect to causative (लुङ् लकार) श्वि dhātu, viz. अशूसुवत, अशिश्वियत् quote Pāribhāṣika 106 (सम्प्रसारणं सम्प्रसारणाश्रयं च बलीयो भवति) at following derivational step:

श्वि इ(णिच्) अ(चङ्) त्

Note: - Here sūtra णौ च संश्चङोः 6.1.31 teaches सम्प्रसारण optionally.

P-28: - कृद् ग्रहणे गतिकारकपूर्वस्यापि ग्रहणं भवति।।

जहां कृत्प्रत्यय के ग्रहण से कार्य हो, वहां उस कृदन्त के पूर्व गतिसंज्ञक और कारक हो तो भी वह कार्य हो जावे।

[Meaning] Where there is action due to kṛtpratyaya, then even if that kṛt ending item is preceded by gatisañjaka or a kāraka, that action takes place.

P-66: - गतिकारकोपपदानां कृद्भिः सह समाकनचनं प्राक सुबुत्पत्तेः।

गति, कारक और उपपद इन का कृदन्त के साथ सु आदि की उत्पत्ति से पहिले ही समास हो जाता है।

[Meaning] Gati, kāraka and upapada are compounded with words that end in kṛt pratyayas, before the application of su, etc.

Maharshi Dayanand's explanation of these Paribhāṣās is given below:

"यहां केवल सुप् रहित कृदन्त के साथ समास हुआ, तो 'अतिङ्' ग्रहण सार्थक होने से स्वार्थ सें चरितार्थ हो गया। और अन्यत्र फल यह है कि गति – 'सांकूटिनम्' यहां जो तद्धितोत्पत्ति से पहिले सम् और कूटिन् सुबन्तों का समास करके पीछे तद्धित उत्पन्न किया चाहें, तो तद्धितोत्पत्ति की विवक्षा में कूटिन् शब्द की पृथक् प्रातिपादिक संज्ञा रहने से सम् शब्द को वृद्धि नहीं हो सकती। और जब सुप् रहित केवल कूटिन् कृदन्त के साथ समास होता है, तब समास समुदाय की एक प्रातिपादिक संज्ञा होकर तद्धितोत्पत्ति होने से 'सम्' को वृद्धि हो जाती है।"

[Meaning] Here it is componded only with the kṛdanta without sup, then admission of 'atiṅga', being meaningful, has operated automatically. And elsewhere the result is that before तद्धित operation when सम (गति संज्ञा) and कूटिन् (सुबन्त) are compounded, then कूटिन् being designated with a separate prātipadika sañjñā, सम cannot admit vṛddhi and when कूटिन् without sup affix is compounded with कृदन्त, the whole compounded word is designated as prātipadika and सम does not admit vṛddhi on तद्धित operation

Let us understand this by derivation of सांकूटिनाम्

Example: 6

कूट (दाहे)	भूवादयो धातवः (3.1.1), अभिविधौ भाव इनुण् (3.3.44).
कूट+इनुण (इन)	कुगतिप्रादयः (2.2.18) teaches compounding of कूट्+इन
सम कूट् इन	कृत्तद्धितसमासाश्च (1.246), अणिनुणः (5.4.15), प्रत्ययः (3.1.1) परश्च (3.1.2).

Here कूटिन् is derived from कूट dhātu, if we do समास of सम and कूटिन् after considering them as सुबन्त pada (सम+सु+कूटिन्+सु) and subsequently do the तद्धित operation then सम and कूटिन् will be treated as separate प्रातिपादिक. In that case, वृद्धि operation will not be initiated with respect to सम, instead, it will be operational with respect to कूटिन्.

Therefore, in case of सम (गति संज्ञा) and कूटिन् (कृदन्त), समास occurs only between compounds which are not सुप्. Now compound of समकूटिन् will be treated as a single प्रातिपादिक and this will entail तद्धित operation and thus वृद्धि operations are performed on सम instead of कूटिन्. Thus, we arrive at

	the next form.
	सम् कूट् इन् अण् नस्तद्धिते (6.4.144) entails लोप of टि portion. Sūtra इनण्यनपत्ये (6.4.164) assign प्रकृतिभाव and restricts लोप operation. By sūtra तद्धितेष्वाचामादेः (7.2.117) मोऽनुस्वारः (7.1.24) we arrive at next step.
सामकूटिन	Now after assigning प्रातिपदिक sañjñā, सु becomes अम् by sūtra अतोऽम् (71.24). On account of पूर्व रुप we arrive at next form.

सामकूटिनम्

In forthcoming examples, for the sake of brevity, we will be obviating various steps which do not have ल impact on derivational function.

Example: (7)

भृञ् (भरणे) dhātu is उभयपदि i.e. It has both परस्मैपद and आत्मनेपद forms. Here we are discussing लट् लकार, third person and singular form.

	परस्मैपद	आत्मनेपद
भूवादयो धातवः (१।३।१)	भृ	भृ
धातोः (३।१।९१) वर्तमाने लट् (३।२।१२३) प्रत्ययः (३।१।१), परश्च (३।१।१)	भृ+ल्	भृ+ल्
लस्य (३।४।७७)	भृ+तिप्	भृ+तिप्
तिप्तस्झिसिप्थस्थमिब्वस्मस्तातांझथाथांध्वमिड्वहिमहिङ्० (३।४।७८	महिङ्	महिङ्

At this stage, three संज्ञा sūtras become applicable: -

1. यस्मात् प्रत्ययविधिस्तदादि प्रत्ययेऽङ्गम्
   (१।४।१३)
2. लः परस्मैपदम् (१।४।१८)
3. तिङ् शित् सार्वधातुकम् (३।४।११३)

Sūtra 1.4.13 and Sūtra 1.4.18 falls within adhikāra of sūtra आ कडारादेका संज्ञा (1.4.1) which extends up to sūtra काडाराः कर्मधारये (2.2.38). Hence between these two, only one sañjñā will be applicable. 1.4.18 being पर sūtra, will be applicable.

3.4.113 is पर and नित्य sūtra.

3.4.113 being नित्य, precedes 1.4.18.

Now तिप्......महिङ् acquire सार्वधातुक संज्ञा (3.4.118) and कर्तरि शप् (३।१।६८) becomes operative.

If we apply शप् at this stage, then we get stuck with further derivation.

For more clarification, refer to point 14, chapter 3.

Paribhāṣā-41 resolves this issue.

विकरणेभ्यो नियमो बलीयान् ।।

विकरण विधि से आत्मनेपद परस्मेपद नियमविधान बलवान् है।

[Meaning] Atmanepada and Parasmepada rule is stronger than vikaraṇa operation.

Ṛṣi Dayanand's explanation: "अब यह विचार भी कर्तव्य है कि धातुओं से परे जो लकारों के स्थान से 'तिप्' आदि परस्मैपद और आत्मनेपद प्रत्यय होते हैं, वे पहिले हों किंवा विकरण हों? आत्मनेपदादि के करने से प्रथम

और पीछे भी विकरणों की प्राप्ति है, इससे वे नित्य हैं और आत्मनेपद परस्मैपद विधायक प्रकरण से परे भी विकरण ही हैं, और विकरण किये पीछे आत्मनेपद नियम की प्राप्ति नहीं, क्योंकि [अनुदात्तङित आत्मनेपदम् (1.3.12)] यह पञ्चमीनिर्दिष्ट कार्य व्यवधानरहित उत्तर को होना चाहिये। विकरणों के व्यवधान से फिर आत्मनेपद नहीं पाता। क्योंकि जो आत्मनेपद आदि के होने से पहिले विकरण ही होते हों, तो [आत्मनेपदेष्वन्यतरस्याम् (3.1.54) पुषादिद्युताद्य्लृदितः परस्मैपदेषु (3.1.55)] इन विकरणविधायक सूत्रों में आत्मनेपद के आश्रय से विकरणविधान क्यों किया?"

[Meaning] Now it is also a point to think whether the parasmaipada and ātmanepada suffixes are to be applied first to dhātus or vikaraṇas? Vikaraṇas can be applied before and after applying ātmanepada, etc. suffixes, so they are nitya and vikaraṇas are also taught after the rules teaching operation of ātmanepada and parasmaipada pratyayas. Moreover, if vikaraṇa is operated first, rules teaching ātmanepada and parasmaipada are blocked, because operation by *anudāttaṅgit atmanepadam* (1.3.12) is directed in the ablative case, so it is to be applied to immediately to the next unintervened by any other pratyayas or item. When there is intervention of vikaraṇa, ātmanepada operation cannot take place, because had the vikaraṇa operation taught before the operation of ātmanepada, etc. there would have not be any provision of vikaraṇa operation based upon ātmanepada etc. taught in the following sūtras:

ātmanepadeshvanyatarsyam (3.1.54)

puṣādidyutādyḷditaḥ parasmaipadeṣu (3.1.55)]

Further Ṛṣi Dayanand states "अङ्ग कार्य से विकरण का होना प्रथम इष्ट है क्योंकि विकरणों के आ जाने पर सब की अङ्ग संज्ञा हो जाती है।"

[Meaning] Vikaraṇa operation is to be accomplished prior to aṅga designation, becasue after vikaraṇa operation is done, all together can be desinated as aṅga.

This Paribhāṣā implies that विकरणs are नित्य and hence precede other operation. However, if विकरण is placed between dhātu and pratyaya, then परस्मैपद and आत्मनेपद operation will be impossible, as sūtra 1.3.12 is in ablative form and teaches operation on dhātu unobstructed by any other pratyaya or item. It further states that after applying rules teaching परस्मैपद and आत्मनेपद, विकरण process will precede other operations, because विकरण along with dhātu will also acquire अङ्ग sañjñā.

Hence before application of शप् pratyaya following संज्ञा sūtras will be applicable:

भृ+ति भृ+त

लः परस्मैपदम् (1.4.98)

Its अपवाद sūtra **तङानावात्मनेपदम्** (1.4.99) is applicable for आत्मनेपद.

According to स्वरितञितः कर्त्रभिप्राये क्रियाफले (1.3.72) भृ dhātu is both ātmanepadi and prasamaipadi.

For परस्मैपद sūtra शेषात्कर्तरि परस्मेपदम् (1.3.78) and for आत्मनेपद sūtra अनुदात्तङित आत्मनेपदम् (1.3.12) will be applicable.

Subsequently following sūtras will follow:

तिङस्त्रीणि त्रीणि प्रथममध्यमोत्तमाः (१।४।१००)

शेषे प्रथमः (१।४।१०७)
तान्येकवचन द्विवचनबहुवचनान्येकशः(१।४।१०१)

द्व्येकयोर्द्विवचनैकवचने (1।४।२२)

Above sūtras teach तिप् and त for

परस्मैपद and आत्मनेपद, respectively.

After completion of above process, we can apply यस्मात् प्रत्ययविधिस्तदादि प्रत्ययेऽङ्गम् (१।४।१३) and तिङ् शित् सार्वधातुकम् (३।४।११३), as both the sañjñās are out of purview of 1.4.1 hence both are applicable. Due to this fact शप्, ति and त acquires सार्वधातुक् sañjñā. भृ+शप्+ति भृ+शप्+त

Since both the sūtras are नित्य, पर sūtra 3.4.113 will precede and this will entail operation of कर्तरि शप् (३।१।६८).

Now भृ will become अङ्ग of शप् and शप् will become अङ्ग of ति and त, while भृ and शप् will become अङ्ग of ति and त.

Example: (8)

चिती संज्ञाने dhātu is परस्मैपदी, here we are discussing लिट् लकार, third person, singular form:

(Please note that for the sake of brevity, steps that have already been discussed will not be repeated here)

लस्य (३।४।७७) चित्+तिप्...महिङ्

तिप्तस्झिसिप्थस्थमिब्वस्मस्तातांझथाथांध्वमिड्वहिमहिङ्० (३।४।७८)

At this stage following sañjñā and vidhi sūtras become applicable: चित्+तिप्...महिङ्

ल: परस्मैपदम् (१।४।९८)

Now sūtra ल: परस्मैपदम् (1.4.98) assign परस्मैपद sañjñā, अपवाद sūtra

परस्मैपदानां णलतुसुस्थलथुसणल्वमाः(3.4.82)

becomes applicable.

After application of sūtras related to परस्मैपद, एकवचन्, etc. we get	चित्+णल्
Now following sañjñā and विधि sūtras are applicable:	
यस्मात् प्रत्ययविधिस्तदादि प्रत्ययेऽङ्गम् (१।४।१३)	
तिङ् शित् सार्वधातुकम् (३।४।११३)	
लिट् च (3.4.115) sūtra is अपवाद of sūtra 3.4.113 and assign आर्धधातुक sañjñā.	
लिटि धातोरनभ्यास्य (6.1.8) is नित्य sūtra which reduplicate चित्.	
Since णल् is आर्धाधतुक् and चित् acquire अङ्ग sañjñā, hence will entail the application of पुगन्तलघुपधस्य च (7.3.86) and will initiate गुण operation. Sūtra (6.1.8) is पूर्व and नित्य, while sūtra 7.3.86 is पर and नित्य.	चेत्+णल
Since both are नित्य, but 7.386, being पर sūtra, will entail गुण of चित् and thereafter, reduplication sūtras will be applicable.	
We will have steps stated in the right hand column.	
After the application of the above steps, we will have the form depicted in the right hand column. (This form is obtained after the application of अभ्यास् sūtras.)	चिचेत

Example: (9)

भू	भूवादयो०, धातोः, अनद्यतने लङ् (३।२।१११),

भू लङ्	At this step, following the derivational process mentioned in examples 1 & 2, i.e., designation of आत्मनेपद, etc., we arrive at the next step:
भू तिप्	Now at this step, due to अङ्ग sañjñā, शप् is applicable before तिप्.

While अट्, by virtue of sūtra लुङ लङ्लृङ् क्ष्वडुदात्तः (६।४।७१) is to be prefixed to भू due by virtue of sūtra आद्यन्तौ टकितौ (१।१।४५).

Both the sūtras are नित्य, hence परत्व sūtra 6.4.71 is applicable.

Paribhāṣā 41 states that विकरण process is to be done before अङ्ग process because after the application of विकरण, भू+शप् will acquire अङ्ग sañjñā.

Hence, now sūtra 6.4.71 will be applicable to the conjugation भू+शप् and so अट् will be prefixed to this conjugation.

In the context of Paribhāṣā 42, Maharshi Dayanand explains the application of अट् and विकरण as below:

Paribhāṣā-42: शब्दान्तरस्य च प्राप्नुवन् विधिरनित्यो भवति।।

"जो दो कार्य एक साथ प्राप्त हो, और वे दोनों नित्य ठहरते हों, तो उनमें एक विधि के होने से पहिले जिस शब्द को दूसरी विधि प्राप्त है, और पहिले कार्य के होने के पश्चात वह विधि दूसरे शब्द को प्राप्त हो,

तो वह अनित्य होता है।".

It implies that previously अट् was applicable to अङ्ग 'भू' of भू+तिप् and शप् too was applicable at this step. At this step, the application of both is नित्य, but after the application of शप् pratyaya, अट् is now applicable to भू+शप्. This changes the applicability of अट् and thus renders अट् as अनित्य in comparison to the previous position.

From this, it is concluded that after the application of विकरण, अट् pratyaya remains applicable.

After application of विकरण, नित्य sūtra इतश्च (३।४।१००) is applied and we arrive at next step

अट् भवत् = अभवत्

Example: (10) कमु कान्तौ (इच्छा)

Here we are discussing the form of लुङ् लकार.

कम्+णिङ् कम dhātu acquires णिङ् pratyaya when it depicts it own meaning.

Subsequently, due to अन्तरङ्ग sūtra अत उपधायाः 7.2.116 and बहिरङ्ग sūtra सनाद्यन्ता धातवः, we arrive at the next step:

कामि Since णिङ् pratyaya is ङित्व; hence आत्मनेपद pratyaya is applicable and by application of विकरण taught by sūtra णिश्रिद्रुस्रुभ्यः कर्तरि चङ् (3.1.58) which is अपवाद of सिच्, we arrive at the next step:

अट+काम्+इ+अ(चङ्)+त

At this step, by sūtra णेरनिटि (6.4.51), लोप of णि is applicable, whereas sūtra अतो लोपः (6.4.48) teaches the लोप of अ (चङ्).

However, on closer examination following sūtras are applicable:

एरनेकाचोऽसंयोगपूर्वस्य (6.4.82) is परत्व sūtra.

अचि श्नुधातुभ्रुवां य्वोरियङुवङौ (6.4.77) पूर्व sūtra with respect to 6.4.82 but पर with respect to 6.4.51 and 6.4.48.

Operation of सार्वधातुकार्धधातुकयोः (7.3.84) is restricted due to ङित् nature of अङ्

Sūtra 6.4.82 entails (इ+अ) यण् operation while sūtra 6.4.77 entails (इ+अ) इयङ् in place of णिच् (इ)+अङ् (अ).

However, sūtra 6.4.51 is अपवाद sūtra and hence by पूर्वविप्रतिषेध, लोप of णि is done and we arrive at next step. This fact is further corroborated by Paribhāṣā 99 “सर्वविधिभ्यो लोपविधिर्बलियान्” i.e., लोप process is stronger than other process.

अट्+काम्+चङ्+त

By sūtra णौ चङ् युपधाया ह्रस्वः (7.4.1), we arrive at the next step

अट+कम्+चङ्+त

By sūtra चङि (6.1.11), we have the next step

अट्+कम्+कम्+चङ्+त (Here कम् is reduplicated)

By sūtra सन्वल्लघुनि चङ् परेऽनग्लोपे (7.4.93), operation akin to सन् pratyaya is accomplished. Here it is to be noted that due to the treatment of णिलोप as स्थानिवत्, this sūtra is applicable. Afterwords, sūtra सन्यतः 7.4.79, becomes applicable and we arrive at the following step

अट्+किम्+कम्+चङ्+त

At this step, by sūtra दीर्घो लघोः (7.4.94), कुहोश्चुः (7.4.62) and हलादिः शेषः (7.4.60), we arrive at the following step:

अट्+ची+कम्+अ+त = अचीकमत

In case of non-application of णिङ् pratyaya, वार्तिक 3.1.84 कमेरूपसङ्ख्यानम् with कम dhātu in place of च्लि चङ् pratyaya is applies, consequent upon which we have the next step:

अट्+कम्+चङ्+त = अचकमत

Here by परत्व sutra अचिश्नुधातुभ्रुवां य्वोरियङुवङौ (6.4.77) is applicable.

Foregoing examples prove that Ārṣa-vidhi is an inevitable and integral part of the Pāṇinian system.

Chapter-6

Ārṣa-vidhi vis-a-vis C-process

I. नामिक (Nominal Inflection)

1. देव + भिस्

Apavāda sūtra अतो भिस् ऐस् (7.1.9) is applicable.

It is to be noted that in the case of Vedic usage taught by sūtra **बहुलं छन्दसि (7.1.10), ऐस्** is alternatively applicable; hence we also have देवेभिः in addition to देवैः.

By sūtra **नेदमदसोरकोः (7.1.11)** operation of sūtra 7.1.9 is blocked and we have following forms एभिः and अमीभिः for इदम् and अदस् in place of ऐः (अ+भिस्) and अदैः (अद(स्)+भिस्) respectively.

These forms prove the inefficacy of DOI/SOI operations of the C-process.

2. हरि+टा

Ancient tradition ascribes आङ् for टा; accordingly, Maharshi Pāṇini has used both names.

आङो नास्त्रियाम् (7.3.119), being पर and also being अपवाद sūtra, is applicable.

3. वारि+टा

आङो नास्त्रियाम् (7.3.119), being पर and also being अपवाद sūtra, is applicable.

4. स्त्री+आम्

ह्रस्वनद्यापो नुट् (7.1.54), being पर sūtra, is applicable.

5. वारि+आम्

By virtue of vārttika नुमचिरतृज्वद्भावेभ्यो नुट् पूर्वविप्रतिषेधेन application of नुट् precede over application of नुम्, for explanation see point no. 3 of chapter no. 4.

6. क्रोष्टु + आम्

By virtue of vārttika नुमचिरतृज्वद्भावेभ्यो नुट् पूर्वविप्रतिषेधेन, application of विभाषा तृतीयादिष्वचि (7.1.97) is restricted by ह्रस्वनद्यपो नुट् (7.1.54), for explanation see point no. 4 of chapter 4.

7. कर्तृ + सु (neuter gender)

स्वमोर्नपुंसकात् (7.1.23), being अपवाद, is applicable.

8. तद् + सु (neuter gender)

स्वमोर्नपुंसकात् (7.1.23), being अपवाद, is applicable

9. वारि+ङे

इकोऽचि विभक्तौ (7.1.73), being अपवाद is applicable.

10. राजन् + सु

Sūtra सर्वनामस्थाने चासम्बुधौ (6.4.8) and हल्ङ्याब्भ्यो दीर्घात् सुतिस्यपृक्तं हल् (6.1.66) both are नित्य, but sūtra 6.1.88, being अपवाद sūtra, will apply first followed by 6.4.8.

11. त्रि+आम् (neuter gender)

Both sūtras त्रिचतुरोः स्त्रियां तिसृचतसृ (7.2.99) and ह्रस्वनद्यापो नुट् (7.1.54) are नित्य; hence 7.2.99, being पर sūtra, will apply followed by पूर्व sūtra 7.1.54.

12. त्रि+आम् (feminine, genitive)

Both sūtras त्रिचतुरोः स्त्रियां तिसृचतसृ (7.2.99) and ह्रस्वनद्यापो नुट् (7.1.54) are नित्य; hence 7.2.99, being पर, अन्तरङ्ग and अपवाद, will apply first followed by पूर्व sūtra.

13. इदम् + ङे (masculine)

Sūtras त्यादादीनामः (7.2.102) and अनाप्यकः (7.2.112) are नित्य, but 7.2.102, being अन्तरङ्ग, will apply first. In this case we will get:

इद अ +ङे

Here again अतो गुणे (6.1.94), being अन्तरङ्ग, will apply by preceding 7.2.112, and we will have:

इद+ ङे

At this step, अपवाद sūtra सर्वनाम्नः स्मै (7.1.14) will again precede 7.2.112 and we get:

इद + स्मै

At this step, हलि लोपः (7.2.113) which is अपवाद of 7.2.112 will again restrict 7.2.112 and we will have:

अ+स्मै

14. अस्मद्+सु

Sūtra मपर्यन्तस्य (7.2.91) is an adhikāra sūtra which teaches that following sūtras under adhikāra of this sūtra will apply up to म् of अस्मद् and युष्मद्.

Sūtra त्वाहौ सौ (7.2.94), which falls under adhikāra of 7.2.97, following the principle of पूर्व, पर, नित्य with respect to other sūtras, being अपवाद, is applicable; we have the following:

अह+अद+सु

Sūtra शेषे लोपः (7.2.90), being अपवाद, precedes other sūtras and we have

अह + सु

Here it is pertinent to note that applications of sūtra 7.2.94 and 7.2.90 have restricted application of sūtra युष्मदस्मदोरनादेशे (7.2.86) and now it is no more applicable. At this stage, we are left with sūtra ङेप्रथमयोरम् (7.1.28) and we get:

अह+अम्

By applying पूर्वरूपैकादेश (अतो गुणे) sūtra we get the final form अहम्

15. राम+भ्यस् (dative)

Sūtra बहुवचने झल्येत (7.3.103) is पर sūtra with respect to सुपि च (7.3.102), so applicable.

16. वन + सु

Sūtra स्वमोर्नपुंसकात् (7.1.23) is restricted by sūtra अतोऽम् (7.1.24), because it is पर and अपवाद sūtra with respect to 7.1.23.

17. युष्मद्+भ्यस्

पञ्चम्या अत् (7.1.31) is पर and अपवाद sūtra with respect to भ्यसो भ्यम् (7.1.30), hence applicable.

18. एक + ङे

सर्वनाम्नः स्मै (7.1.14) is पर and अपवाद sūtra with respect to ङेर्य (7.1.13), hence applicable.

19. हरि + औ

Sūtra प्रथमयोः पूर्वसवर्णः (6.1.98) is पर sūtra with respect to इको यणचि (6.1.74), hence preferably applicable.

20. वारि + ङि (neuter, locative)

इकोऽचि विभक्तौ (7.1.73) is अपवाद sūtra with respect to औदच्च घेः (7.3.118), hence precedes it.

21. त्रि+आम् (masculine, genitive)

Sūtra त्रेस्त्रयः (7.1.53) is पूर्व with respect to ह्रस्वनद्यापो नुट् (7.1.54) which is पर and नित्य sūtra, but त्रेस्त्रयः (7.1.53) is अन्तरङ्ग, hence it is applicable first followed by 7.1.54.

22. भवत्+सु

भवत् is derived from 'भा' दिप्तौ धातु (verbal base) when डवतुप् pratyaya taught by भातेर्डवतुप् (उणा-1.63) is placed after it. Vārttika "डित्यभस्यापि टेर्लोपः" teaches लोप of टि part (आ) of भा. As such we get भवत् prātipadika.

In case of भवत्+सु, sūtras अत्वसन्तस्य चाधातोः (6.4.14) and उगिदचाम सर्वनामस्थानेऽधातोः (7.1.70) are applicable. Here sūtra 7.1.70 is पर and नित्य; hence नुम् is to be augmented before the application of 6.4.14. But in this situation दीर्घ of अस् cannot be done. To resolve this problem, Kāśikā, suggests नुम् augment after दीर्घ विधि so that नुम् does not bar दीर्घ विधि.

However, on closer analysis and keeping in mind that vārttika has limited application and Pāribhāṣā has a wider one, it is observed that दीर्घ विधि is अन्तरङ्ग with respect to नुम् आगम् (augment), hence it applies first followed by the sūtra 7.1.70.

II. तद्धित (Secondary Verbal Derivatives), समास (Compounds) and कृदन्त (Primary Verbal Derivatives)

1. प्रति+अच्+ङस्

Due to application of क्विन् pratyaya at initial step, we get प्रति+अच्+ङस्. At this stage of derivation प्रति+अच् is designated as प्रातिपादिक by the sūtra कृत्तद्धितसमासाश्च (1.2.46); hence यण् sandhi is applicable between 'इ' of प्रति and 'अ' of अच्, but due to 'भ' aṅga sañjñā, अपवाद sūtra अचः (6.4.138) elides अ of अच् (अञ्च्) at the end of भ अङ्ग (stem):

प्रति+च्+ङस्

Now sūtra चौ (6.3.137) becomes applicable, as 'च' in this sūtra is remnant of अच् (अञ्चु) and we get प्रतीच्+ङ्

2. सद्+वस्+ङस्

Since the operation of सम्प्रसारण or operation induced by it gains precedence and blocks the application of इड् आगम्, hence we arrive at the following step:

सद्+उस्+ङस्

3. गर्गाः

The derivational equation is noted below:

गर्गस्य गोत्रापत्यानि बहूनि-

गर्ग+ङस्

गर्ग +ङस्+यञ् (समर्थानां प्रथमाद्वा 4.1.82; तस्यापत्यम् 4.1.92; गर्गादिभ्यो यञ् 4.1.105)

गर्ग+य (सुपो धातुप्रातिपदिकयोः 2.4.71)

गर्ग+य+जस् (कृत्तद्धितसमासाश्च (1.2.46)
(स्वौजसमौट्छष्टाभ्याम्भिस्ङेभ्याम्भ्यस्ङसिभ्याम्भ्यस्ङसो साम्ङ्योस्सुप् 4.1.2)

गर्ग+जस् (यञोश्च 2.4.64, being अपवाद sūtra, will block operations of other sūtras)

However, if we wish to derive singular or dual nominative forms, then we will have to apply सु or औ pratyayas instead of जस् pratyaya and we will have the next step:

गर्ग+य+सु (औ) Sūtra 2.4.64 is applicable only in case of the plural form. Since सु and औ are singular and dual form, so this sūtra is not applicable. By sūtra तद्धितेष्वाचामादेः (7.2.117), we will have the next step

गार्ग्यः, गार्ग्यौ

Now let us discuss the derivation of गार्गीयाः

गार्गीयाः

The derivational equation is appended noted below:

गर्गणाम् छात्राः- गर्ग+ङस्+यञ्...गर्ग+य...गर्ग+य+आम्.. is the derivational form of गर्गणाम्, plural genitive case.

गर्ग+य+आम् (As at next step pratyaya beginning with vowel sound is expected; hence sūtra गोत्रेऽलुगचि 4.1.89 will become operational and block लुक operation of sūtra यञोश्च 2.4.64)

Note: - In derivation of लुट् लकार of दीङ् क्षये dhātu, same principle is followed when sūtra मीनातिमिनोतिदीङां ल्यपि च

	(6.1.49) becomes operational, at the next step long vowel एच् is expected. Maharshi Patañjali too discusses this operational sequence, which C-process failed to comprehend. Even Maharshi Dayanand has stated the same fact, which we have mentioned at point no-11.
गार्ग्य+आम्	(तद्धितेष्वचामादेः 7.2.117)
गार्ग्य+आम्+छ	(वृद्धाच्छः 4.2.113, सुपो धातुप्रातिपदिकयोः 2.4.71)
गार्ग्य+छ	By sūtra आयनेयीनीयियः फढखछघां प्रत्ययादीनाम् (7.1.2), यस्येति च (6.4.148) कृत्तद्धितसमासाश्च (1.2.46), (स्वौजसमौट्छष्टाभ्याम्भिस्ङेभ्याम्भ्यस्ङसिभ्याम्भ्यस्ङसो साम्ङ्योस्सुप् 4.1.2), we arrive at the next step:
गार्ग्य्+ईय+जस्	

However, C-process derived singular form of (गर्गस्य गोत्रापत्यम् = गार्ग्यः), गार्गस्येमे छात्राः इति **गार्गीयाः.**

The derivational steps for it will be as under:

गार्ग्यस्य छात्राः	गर्ग+ङस्....गर्ग+ङस्+यञ्....गर्ग+यञ्+ङस् is the derivational form for singular genitive case.
गर्ग+ङस्+यञ्	By application of sūtra 2.4.71 we arrive at the next step:
गर्ग+यञ्	By (तद्धितेष्वचामादेः 7.2.117), आयनेयीनीयियः फढखछघां प्रत्ययादीनाम् (7.1.2), यस्येति च (6.4.148) कृत्तद्धितसमासाश्च (1.2.46), we

arrive at next step:

Since it is a singular form; hence sūtra 2.4.64 will not be applicable.

गार्ग्+य+छ+जस् गार्ग्य+ईय+जस्......गार्गीयाः

From the above steps, it is clear that in the derivation of गार्ग्यस्य छात्राः sūtra 2.4.64 becomes redundant.

But, C-process has adopted this step, thus proving that it has blindly followed Kaumudi which has clouded its logic with utter confusion.

4. पञ्चालः

Derivational equation is given below:

पञ्चाल + ङस् (समर्थानां प्रथमाद्वा 4.1.82, तस्यापत्यम् 4.1.92, जनपदशब्दात् क्षत्रियाजञ् 4.1.166)

पञ्चाल+ङस्+अञ् (सुपो धातुप्रातिपदिकयोः 2.4.71)

पञ्चाल + अञ् (ते तद्राजाः 4.1.172, तद्राजस्य बहुषु तैनैवास्त्रियाम् 2.4.62) तद्राजस्य बहुषु तैनैवास्त्रियाम् 2.4.62, being अपवाद sūtra, will block other sūtras and लुक will precede.

5. पुष्यः

The derivational equation is given below:

पुष्येण युक्तः कालः

पुष्य+टा+अण् (लुबविशेषे 4.2.4, नक्षत्रेण युक्तः कालः 4.2.3)

4.2.4 being पर and अपवाद sūtra, लुप् process will operate.

पुष्य+सु (कृत्तद्धितसमासाश्च (1.2.46)

6. पञ्चमः

The derivational equation is noted below: -

पञ्चानां पूरणं -

पञ्चन्+ आम्+ डट् (सुपो धातुप्रातिपदिकयोः 2.4.71)

पञ्चन्+डट् (नान्तादसङ्ख्यादेर्मट् 5.2.49, being अपवाद and पर sūtra, will block other operations and मट् āgama will prefix डट्)

पञ्चन्+मट्+डट्

III. आख्यातिक (Verbal inflection)

1. एध्+झ (Present, third person, plural)

Refer to point no. 14, page chapter 4.

Before application of sūtra 3.1.68, application of तिप्...महिङ् into आत्मनेपदि and परस्मैपदि is must. Thereafter नित्य sūtra 3.1.68 will become applicable and we will arrive at the following step:

एध्+शप्+झ

After performing इत् and लोप operations, we arrive at the following form:

एध्+अ+झ

At this stage following two sūtras are applicable:

झोऽन्तः (7.1.3) and टित आत्मनेपदानां टेरे (3.4.79). Both are नित्य, hence पर 7.1.3 will apply first followed by 3.4.79 sūtra. We will arrive at following derivational step:

एध्+अ+अन्ते

2. धा+झि (Present, third person, plural)

धा+शप्+झि	At this step, अपवाद sūtra जुहोत्यादिभ्यः श्लुः (2.4.75) teaches अदर्शन of शप् pratyaya. We will have following form:
धा+झि	At this step two sūtras are applicable- श्लौ (6.1.10) and झोऽन्तः (7.1.3). Here झोऽन्तः (7.1.3) is अन्तरङ्ग sūtra, but श्लौ, being अपवाद sūtra, will apply first. Sūtra 6.1.10 teaches reduplication of धा dhātu when श्लौ occurs. **At this step, if we follow the C-process, then due to DOI operation, 7.1.3 will apply, consequent upon which we will arrive at an impossible form धा+अन्ति**
धा धा+झि	At this step, the reduplicated form of दा दा will acquire अभ्यस्त sañjñā by application of sūtra उभे अभ्यस्तम् (6.1.5). On application of Sūtra 6.1.5 following sūtras will become applicable: श्नाभ्यस्तयोरातः (6.4.112), झोऽन्तः (7.1.3) and अदभ्यस्तात् (7.1.4). Since, sūtra 7.1.4 is अपवाद sūtra, it will precede other sūtras and blocks application of sūtra 7.1.13 and thereafter नित्य sūtra 6.4.112 will apply and we will arrive at the following step:
धा ध्+अति	After application of other sūtras of अभ्यास् we will arrive at **दधति** form.

3. हा+तस् (Present, third person, dual)

C-process committed the same mistake as was done in the derivation of दा+झि. In continuation of the process applied in example 2, we get

हा हा+तस्	At this step sūtra जहातेश्च (6.4.116) and ई हल्यघोः (6.4.113) are applicable. Since 6.4.116 is applied alternately/ optionally, hence we arrive at the following two steps:
हा ही+तस्	On application of जहातेश्च (6.4.116)
हा हि+तस्	On application of ई हल्यघोः (6.4.113)

4. वप्+त (लङ् कर्मणि, Imperfect passive, third person, singular)

वप्+त	At this step, sūtras 3.4.113 and 1.4.13 teach सार्वधातुक and अङ्ग sañjñā of त and also त is designated ङित् by sūtra सार्वधातुकमपित् (1.2.4). After the application of the above-mentioned sūtras, the following sūtras become operational. सार्वधातुके यक् (3.1.67), वचिस्वपियजादिनां किति (6.1.15), लुङ्लङ्लृङ्क्ष्वडुदात्तः (6.4.71). Here 3.1.67 is पूर्व and अपवाद; 6.1.15 is पर and अन्तरङ्ग and 6.4.71 is पर and नित्य. 3.1.67, being अपवाद, will apply first and we will arrive at the following step:
वप्+यक्+त	At this step, यक् being कित्, 6.1.15 is

applicable. Since sūtra 6.4.71 teaches अङ्ग संज्ञा, so applicable. 6.1.15, being अन्तरङ्ग, precedes 6.4.71 which is नित्य. After completion of सम्प्रसारण operation, we will arrive at the following step:

उप+यक्+त	Now at this step due to सम्प्रसारण operation, we will have आडजादीनाम् (6.4.72) applicable, which is अपवाद of 6.4.71 which is also applicable being नित्य, but its operation is blocked by its अपवाद sūtra 6.4.72.

Here paribhāṣā sūtras-41, 42 and 106 are relevant which have already been discussed. It is also to be noted that the role of paribhāṣā is to decide the outcome pending contradiction.

5. श्वि+त्त्वा

श्वि + त्त्वा	At this step, त्त्वा pratyaya, being कित्वत् and also being अङ्ग with respect to त्त्वा, allows following sūtras to be applicable:

वचिस्वपियजादिनां किति (6.1.15), आर्धधातुकस्येड् वलादेः (7.2.35), पुगन्तलघुपधस्य च (7.3.84).

6.1.15 is पूर्व and नित्य; 7.2.35 is पर and नित्य; 7.3.84 is पर with respect to 6.1.15 and 7.2.35. Sūtra 6.1.15 and 7.2.35 being नित्य with respect to 7.3.84 will precede it. But sūtra 7.2.35, being पर sūtra with respect to 6.1.15 will precede it. We will have following step:

श्वि+इट्+त्त्वा — At this step, 6.1.15, being नित्य, becomes applicable, but simultaneously न त्त्वा सेट (1.2.18), being पूर्व, अपवाद and निषेध sūtra, also becomes applicable.

At this step Paribhāṣā-98 "प्रतिषेधाश्च बलीयांसो भवन्ति" states that प्रतिषेध is more powerful than पर, नित्य and अन्तरङ्ग sūtras. Therefore sūtra 1.2.18 will block operations arising due to कित्वत् nature of त्त्वा and thus sūtra 6.1.15 will become defunct and now अङ्ग sañjñā sūtra 7.3.84 will become applicable.

6. हन्+क्त

हन्+क्त — At this step, sūtras अनुनासिकस्य क्विझलोः क्ङिति (6.4.15) and अनुदात्तोपदेशवनतितनोत्यादीनामनुनासिक लोपो झलि क्ङिति (6.4.37) are applicable. 6.4.37 being पर sūtra will be applicable.

7. हन्+झि (Present, third-person, plural)

हन्+झि — At this step, sūtras अनुनासिकस्य क्विझलोः क्ङिति (6.4.15), अनुदात्तोपदेशवनतितनोत्या-दीनामनुनासिक लोपो झलि क्ङिति (6.4.37) and झोऽन्तः (7.1.3) are applicable.

Sūtra 7.1.3, being नित्य, will be applicable and at the next step we will have the following equation:

हन्+अन्ति — At this step, गमहनजनखनघसां लोपः क्ङित्यनङि (6.4.98) becomes applicable due to presence of अजादि pratyaya and we will arrive at following step:

ह् न्+अन्ति — At this step, हो हन्तेर्ञ्णिन्नेषु (7.3.54) becomes applicable due to absence of vowel between ह् and न् and we will arrive at the following step:

घ्न्+अन्ति

8. क्रम्+त्त्वा

क्रम+त्वा — The verbal root is क्रमु in which उ vowel is elided being इत्. Consequent upon which अपवाद sūtra उदितो वा (7.2.56) will precede. Since this sūtra prohibits the application of इट् optionally, hence निषेध (prohibition), being more powerful, will apply first and we will have the following equation:

क्रम्+त्वा — At this step, क्रमश्च त्क्वि (6.4.18) will be applicable and as it optionally teaches elongation of उपधा i.e. penultimate vowel, again निषेध (prohibition) option will precede and we will have the following step:

क्रम्+त्वा

As the option of निषेध (prohibition) operation of 6.4.18, we will have next step:

क्राम्+त्वा

As the option of निषेध taught by 7.2.56, we will have the following step:

क्रम्+इट्+त्वा

9. अतिक्रम्+त्त्वा

अतिक्रम्+त्त्वा At this step, according to the paribhāṣā-48 "अन्तरङ्गानपि विधीन् बहिरङ्गो ल्यब् बाधते" application of ल्यप् pratyaya will block all the operations arising due to त्त्वा pratyaya and we will arrive at the next step:

अतिक्रम्+ल्यप्

10. प्रस्था+त्त्वा

प्रस्था+ल्यप् Paribhāṣā-48 "अन्तरङ्गानपि विधीन् बहिरङ्गो ल्यब् बाधते" will apply

11. आगम्+त्त्वा

आगम्+ल्यप् Here also paribhāṣā-48 "अन्तरङ्गानपि विधीन् बहिरङ्गो ल्यब् बाधते" will apply

12. प्र+वेञ+त्त्वा

प्रवे।ल्याप् Paribhāṣā-48 "अन्तरङ्गानपि विधीन् बहिरङ्गो ल्यब् बाधते" will apply

In all the above-cited examples ल्यप् by virtue of स्थानिवत् (similar to substituted one) will be treated as कित्वत्, besides it also blocks operations of त्त्वा.

Here it is pertinent to mention that C-process has acted in contravention of its premises which have been highlighted by us at points no. 14, 15 and 19 in chapter 3 and did not carry out operations arising due to त्त्वा pratyaya before replacement with ल्यप्.

13. शस्+सिप् (लोट् or Imperative, second person, singular)

शस्+सिप	अपवाद sūtra अदिप्रभृतिभ्यः शपः (2.4.72) teaches लुक् of शप्, as a result, we have this step. Now नित्य sūtra सेर्ह्यपिच्च (3.4.87) becomes applicable and we arrive at the following step.
शास्+हि	At this step, तुह्योस्तातङाशिष्यन्यतरस्याम् (7.1.35) teaches optional replacement of हि with तातङ्. Since निषेध option is more powerful, hence we will first apply निषेध option. As such हुझल्यभ्यो हेर्धिः (6.4.101), teaching replacement of हि pratyaya with धि when हि is preceded by verbal root ending in झल्, will apply and we arrive at the next step:
शा+धि	At this step, शा हौ (6.4.35) teaching replacement of शास् with शा when verbal root is followed by हि, becomes operational, but because of धि it cannot operate. Here both the sūtras 6.4.101 and 6.4.35 have 'prakṛti' (verbal root) as common āśraya (cause or place of action), and both are within the ambit of 6.4.22 असिद्धवदत्राभात्. As such, the operation of para sūtra (6.4.101) will be deemed

suspended and operation taught by pūrva sūtra 6.4.35 will take place and we will arrive at the following:

शा+धि

Now, 7.1.35, being पर and अपवाद with respect to other sūtras, will precede and we will arrive at the following step:

शास्+तात् — तातङ् pratyaya, being ङित्, sūtra शास् इदङ्हलोः (6.4.34) will become applicable and due to absence of हि, 6.4.35 will not be applicable, as such we will arrive at the following step.

शिस्+तात्

14. हन्+सिप् (Imperative, second-person, singular)

हन्+सिप् — अपवाद sūtra अदिप्रभृतिभ्यः शपः (2.4.72) teaches लुक् of शप् and we arrive at this step. Now नित्य sūtra सेर्ह्यपिच्च (3.4.87) becomes applicable and we arrive at the following step:

हन्+हि — At this step, following alternate option of निषेध taught by तुह्योस्तातङ्ङाशिष्यन्यतरस्याम् (7.1.35), अपवाद sūtra हन्तेर्जः (6.4.36) will precede and we will get the following at next step

ज+हि

At this step, अतो हेः (6.4.105) teaching लुक् of हि is applicable in view of the presence of ज, but since both the sūtras (6.4.36 and 6.4.105) are within the jurisdiction of 6.4.22, operation of 6.4.36 will be deemed like असिद्ध (unknown) and 6.4.105 will see हन् and not ज. Thus, sūtra 6.4.105 will not be applicable and we will retain the same form:

ज+हि

In case of optional application of 7.1.35, since तातङ् pratyaya is ङित्, अनुदात्तोपदेशवनतितनेत्यादीनामनुनासिकलोपो झलि क्ङिति (6.4.37) will apply and we will arrive at the following step:

ह+तात्

15. रध्+णिच् (प्रेरणार्थक or Causative present, third person, singular

रध्+णिच् At this step, रध् is अङ्ग with respect to णिच् pratyaya and रध्+णिच् by virtue of सनाद्यन्ता धातवः acquires dhātu sañjñā. Since अङ्ग operation is अन्तरङ् while धातु sañjñā operation is नित्य, so अङ्ग operation will precede. Now sūtra रधिजभोरचि (7.1.61), being अपवाद, will block sūtra अत उपधायाः (7.2.116). At the next step we will have following form

रन्धि Now at this step, धातु sañjñā will become effective and after choosing categories of परस्मैपद, आत्मनेपद, etc. we will arrive at the following step:

रन्धि+तिप्

16. ग्लै+तिप् (Present, third person, singular)

ग्लै+तिप् — At this step, by virtue of paribhāṣā 41, कर्तरि शप् (3.1.68) will precede because after insertion of शप्, ग्लै+शप् will assume अङ्ग sañjñā, whereas, prior to it, only ग्लै was having अङ्ग sañjñā. Thus 3.1.68 teaches अङ्ग संज्ञा of whole set of pratyayas and so will precede आदेच उपदेशेऽशिति (6.1.45) and we will arrive at the following step:

ग्लै+शप्+तिप्

17. दृश्+तुमुन्

दृश्+तुमुन् — सृजिदृशोर्झल्यमकिति (6.1.57), being अपवाद, will be applicable.

18. भू+तिप् (लुङ् or Aorist, third person, singular)

भू+तिप् — At this step, we hope that readers would have developed understanding about application of विकरण and applicability of पूर्व, पर, नित्य, अन्तरङ्ग and अपवाद sūtras. Hence now onward, we will not delve into their application and will proceed with the derivation by hinting at the process. By virtue of sūtras इतश्च (3.4.100) and च्लेः सिच् (3.1.44), we will arrive at the next step.

भू+सिच्+त् — At this step, अपवाद sūtra to 3.1.44, i.e. गातिस्थाघुपाभूभ्यः सिचः परस्मैपदेषु (2.4.77)

will become applicable. We will have the following step:

भू+त्

Here, it is pertinent to note that C-process conceives application of operations initiated by लुक pratyaya considering it स्थानिवत्. For more clarification, refer to points no. 14 to 16 in chapter 3. Here vārttika "आहि भूवोरीद्गतिषेधः" teaches that in case आह् आदेश and after भू स्थानिवत्, function of सिच् does not take place which has been elided.

At this step, अपवाद sūtra भूसुवोस्तिङि (7.3.88) will block गुण operation initiated due to तिप्. Now लुङ्लङ्लृङ्क्ष्वडुदात्तः (6.4.71) will be operational and at next step we will have following equation

अ+भू+त्

19. ग्रह+तिप् **(लुङ्** or Aorist, third person, singular**)**

ग्रह+तिप्

After application of अपवाद sūtra च्लेः सिच् (3.1.44), नित्य sūtra इतश्च (3.4.100) is applied and we arrive at the following step:

ग्रह+सिच्+त्

At this step, अपवाद sūtra ह्म्यन्तक्षणश्वसजागृणिश्व्येदिताम् (7.2.5) becomes applicable followed by नित्य sūtras आर्धातुकस्येड् वलादेः (7.2.35) and अस्तिसिचोऽपृक्ते (7.3.96) and we reach the following step:

ग्रह+इट्+सिच्+ईट्+त् By sūtra लुङ्लङ्लृङ्क्ष्वडुदात्तः (6.4.71) we reach the following step:

अ+ग्रह+इ+स्+ई+त् At this step, इट् ईटि (8.2.28) elides सिच्.

अ+ग्रह+इ+ई+त् Since this sūtra is read within the jurisdiction of पूर्वत्रासिद्धम् (8.2.1), hence it will be treated like असिद्ध (unknown) with respect to दीर्घ operation of इ+ई; hence, we will not be able to do दीर्घ of इ+ई. In this case vārttika सिज्लोप एकादेशे सिद्धो वक्तव्यः resolves the impasse and teaches लोप of सिच् as सिद्ध (known) and thus दीर्घ operation is accomplished. Wc arrive at the following step:

अ+ग्रह+ई+त्

20. गुप्+तिप (Aorist, third person, singular)

गुप्+स्+त् The derivational steps are almost similar as to that of example 19. Here निषेध option taught by sūtra स्वरतिसूतिसूयतिधूञूदितो वा (7.2.44), being more forceful, will apply first followed by the अपवाद sūtra वदव्रजहलन्तस्याचः (7.2.3) and नित्य sūtra अस्तिसिचोऽपृक्ते (7.3.96). Subsequently नित्य sūtra लुङ्लङ्लृङ्क्ष्वडुदात्तः (6.4.71) will become applicable and we will arrive at the following step:

अ+गौप्+स्+ई+त्

In case of augment इट् taught by sūtra

7.2.44, we will have the following:

अ+गुप+स्+त् At this stage, अपवाद sūtra नेटि (7.2.4) blocks operation of 7.2.3 and then पर sūtra पुगन्तलघूपधयस्य च (7.3.86), consequent upon which नित्य sūtra अस्तिसिचोऽपतृक्ते (7.3.96) becomes applicable. Subsequently by virtue of sūtra इट् ईटि (8.2.28) लोप of सिच् is done. As sūtra 8.2.28 falls within adhikāra of 8.2.1, hence by virtue of vārttika सिज्लोप एकादेशे सिद्धो वक्तव्यः, we will have the next step:

अ+गोप्+इ+स+ई+त्

अ+गोप्+ ई+त्

21. भिद्+त (Aorist, third person, singular) (भिदिर् is अनिट् dhātu)

भिद्+त (Refer to examples 18, 19 and 20)

भिद्+स्+त At this step, अपवाद sūtra लिङ्सिचावात्मनेपदेषु (1.2.11) will apply first followed by applications of नित्य sūtra लुङ्लङ्लृङ्क्ष्वडुदात्तः (6.4.71) and पर sūtra पुगन्तलघूपधयस्य च (7.3.86). Subsequently, sūtra झलो झलि (8.2.26) will apply. We will have the following step:

अ+भिद्+त Sūtra 8.2.26 falls within the jurisdiction of adhikāra of 8.2.1, hence by virtue vārttika referred to in examples 18, 19 and 20 सिच् लोप is not असिद्ध (unknown).

22. ऊर्णु+तिप् (लृट् or Simple future, third person, singular)

ऊर्णु+स्य+तिप् At this step, after application of नित्य sūtra आर्धधातुकस्येड् वलादेः (7.2.35), we will apply निषेध option taught by विभाषोर्णोः (1.2.3). Subsequently पर sūtra सार्वधातुकार्धधातुकयोः (7.3.84) will apply. We will arrive at the following stepछ

ऊर्णो+इ+स्य+ति

In case we follow the alternate option taught by 1.2.3 which is अपवाद to the 7.3.84, i.e. अचि श्नुधातुभ्रुवां य्वोरियुङुवङौ (6.4.77), we will reach the following step:

ऊर्णुव्+इ+स्य+ति

23. भू+तिप् (आशीर्लिङ्, Benedictive, third person, singular)

भू+तिप् At this step, अपवाद sūtra यासुट् परस्मैपदेषूदात्तो (3.4.103) and subsequently नित्य सुट् तिथोः (3.4.107) become applicable. Here it is to be noted that 3.4.107 is applicable because of 'त' of लिङ् लकार, whereas sūtra 3.4.103 is applicable because of लिङ् लकार. Hence following the उत्सर्ग-अपवाद principle, these sūtras does not block each other. (Refer to paribhāṣā-43 and 44). Thereafter पूर्व and नित्य sūtra इतश्च (3.4.100) is applicable and we reach the following step:

भू+यास्+स्+त् At this step, sūtras संयोगान्तस्य लोपः (8.2.23) and स्कोः संयोगाद्योरन्ते च (8.2.29) are applicable. Both the sūtras are within the adhikāra of 8.2.1; hence 8.2.23 is applicable. By virtue of vārttika "संयोगादिलोपः संयोगान्तलोपे" application of पर sūtra 8.2.29 is treated as सिद्ध (known) with respect to पूर्व sūtra 8.2.23. Hence sūtra 8.2.29 applies and we obtain the following equation.

भू+या+त्

24. णश(नश्)+तव्यत्

नश्+तव्यत् At this step, following निषेध option taught by sūtra रधादिभ्यश्च (7.2.45), पूर्व sūtra मस्जिनशोर्झलि (7.1.60) becomes applicable and we arrive at the following step:

न न् श्+तव्यत्

In the case of the alternate option taught by पर sūtra 7.2.45, it blocks the operation of 7.1.60 and permit इट् augment between नश्+तव्यत्. Thus, we arrive at the following step:

नश्+इ+तव्यत्

25. तृप्+तुमुन्

तृप्+तुमुन् At this step, should we follow निषेध option taught by sūtra रधादिभ्यश्च

(7.2.45), following two sūtras become applicable.

1. अनुदात्तस्य चर्दुपधस्यान्यतरस्याम् (6.1.58) is पूर्व sūtra and by virtue of it अम् is to be applied optionally. Since निषेध option takes precedence over other options, निषेध option is applied first.

2. पुगन्तलघुपधस्य च (7.3.86) is पर and नित्य sūtra. Following the निषेध option taught by the sūtra 6.1.58, 7.3.86 becomes applicable and we obtain the following step:

तर्प्+तुम्

Should we follow the alternate option taught by 6.1.58, the same occupies the place of अपवाद to sūtra 7.3.86 and blocks its operation. It is also to be noted that after the application of अम्, there will be no इक् available at the penultimate position called उपधा, so we arrive at the following step:

तृ+अम्+प्+तुम्

Should we follow the alternate option taught by 7.2.45; 7.3.86, being पर and नित्य, becomes applicable. Further 7.2.45 will assume the position of पर and अपवाद sūtra and will block the operation of sūtra 6.1.58. As such, we will arrive at the following step:

तर्प+इ+तुम्

26. दिव्+क्त्वा

दिव्+क्त्वा In this case, निषेध option taught by उदितो वा (7.2.56) is applied first. Eventually sūtras च्छ्वोः शूडनुनासिके च (6.4.19) and पुगन्तलघूपधस्य च (7.3.86) become applicable. 7.3.86 is नित्य sūtra while 6.4.19, being अपवाद sūtra, will substitute ऊठ् for व् and we will have the next step:

दि ऊट्+त्वा At this step, on treating व् as स्थानावित्, नित्य sūtra 7.3.86 will be applicable but due to interaction of इ+ऊ, इको यणचि (6.1.74) will be applicable. 6.1.74, being अन्तरङ्ग sūtra, will be applicable and consequently इक् will not be available at the penultimate place. Thus sūtra 7.3.86 will become inoperative and we will have the following step:

द्यू+त्वा

Should we apply alternate option of of 7.2.56, निषेध sūtra न क्त्वा सेट् (1.2.18) will antecede and entail operation by पर sūtra 7.3.86 and we will have the following at next step:

देव्+इ+त्वा

27. खन्+क्त्वा

खन्+क्त्वा At this step, निषेध option taught by

sūtra उदितो वा (7.2.56) will gain precedence and then अपवाद sūtra जनसनखनां सञ्झलो (6.4.42) will become applicable. Here it is worthy to be noted that by मण्डूकपलुति न्याय anuvṛtti of अनुदात्तोपदेशः from sūtra 6.4.37 comes to sūtra 6.4.42. At the next step, we have the following equation:

खा+त्वा

Should we follow the non-निषेध option taught by 7.2.56, due to the augment of इट्, 6.4.42 will be blocked and we arrive at the next step:

खन्+इ+त्वा

28. कृ+सिप्

कृ+सिप् At this step, on application of अपवाद sūtra तनादिकृञ्भ्य उः (3.1.79), नित्य sūtra सेर्ह्यपिच्च (3.4.87) becomes applicable. We will have the following at next step:

कृ+उ+हि At this step, पर and नित्य sūtra सार्वधातुकार्धधातुकयोः (7.3.84) and अपवाद sūtra अत उत सार्वधातुके (6.4.110) become applicable. Sūtra 6.4.110 is पर with respect to अपवाद sūtra उतश्च प्रत्यादसंयोगपूर्वात् (6.4.106) which is पूर्व sūtra. But since sūtra 6.4.110 and 6.4.106 are read within the अधिकार of 6.4.22, so both become applicable.

Now we will have the following at the next step.

कुरु — At this step, by virtue of sūtra हलि च (8.2.77), elongation (दीर्घ) of उ of कु is mandated which is blocked by sūtra न भकुर्छुराम् (8.2.79).

29. अस्+सिप् (लोट्, 'benediction', second person)

अस्+सिप् — At this step, अपवाद sūtra अदिप्रभृतिभ्यः शपः (2.4.72) and नित्य sūtra सेर्ह्यपिच्च (3.4.87) is applicable and we arrive the following at the next step:

अस्+हि — At this step, निषेध option taught by the sūtra तुह्योस्तातङ्ङाशिष्यन्यतरस्याम् (7.1.35) is first applicable. This entails application of the following sūtras:

हुझल्भ्यो हेर्धिः (6.4.101), पूर्व sūtra

श्नसोरल्लोपः (6.4.111), पर and नित्य sūtra

ध्वसोरेद्धावभ्यासलोपश्च (6.4.119), पर and अपवाद sūtra.

But since these sūtras are read under adhikāra of 6.4.22, hence their outcome does not affect each other. By applying 6.4.119 followed by 6.4.111 and latter 6.4.101, we arrive at the next step:

ए+धि

30. भू+त (Passive Aorist, third person, singular; कर्मणि लुङ्)

भू+त

On application of आत्मनेपद् ending taught by भावकर्मणोः (1.3.13) and selecting 'त', etc., endings, following sūtras are applicable:

i. च्लेः सिच् (3.1.44) which is पूर्व and नित्य sūtra.

ii. लुङ्लङ्लृङ्क्ष्वडुदात्तः (6.4.71) which is नित्य sūtra.

6.4.71, being पर sūtra, precede sūtra 3.1.44 but by virtue of paribhāṣā-41, च्लेः सिच् (3.1.44) which teaches substitution of vikaraṇa becomes applicable. Afterwards, चिण् भावकर्मणोः (3.1.66) which is अपवाद of sūtra 3.1.44 will become applicable and we will have the following equation at next step

भू+चिण्+त

Now following sūtras become applicable:

i. सार्वधातुकार्धधातुकयोः (7.3.84), the पर sūtra

ii. अचो ञ्णिति (7.2.115), the अपवाद sūtra.

iii. लुङ्लङ्लृङ्क्ष्वडुदात्तः (6.4.71), the पूर्व and नित्य sūtra

iv. चिणो लुक् (6.4.104), the नित्य and पर sūtra. It is पूर्व sūtra with respect to 7.3.84 and 7.2.115.

Here paribhāṣā-42 is relevant with reference to sūtra 6.4.71, which teaches अट् augment. But after the application of 6.4.104, अट् augment is replaced with चिण्, resulting in

भू+चिण्+त

According to the Ārṣa-vidhi, we apply 7.2.115 first, followed by 6.4.104 and finally 6.4.71 and arrive at the next step:

अ+भौ+इ

31. क्री+झि (Present, third-person, plural)

क्री+झि

After आत्मनेपद, परस्मैपद operation, we will apply sūtra क्र्यादिभ्यः श्ना (3.1.81) introducing विकरण and get the following at next step:

क्री+श्ना+झि

At this step, three sūtras, झोऽन्तः(7.1.3), श्नाभ्यस्तयोरातः (6.4.112) and ई हल्योघोः (6.4.113) are applicable. Of these sūtras:

- 7.1.3 is पर and नित्य and अन्तरङ्ग
- 6.4.113 is अपवाद with respect to sūtra 6.4.112, but sūtra 7.1.3 blocks sūtra 6.4.113.

Hence 6.4.112 and 7.1.3 become applicable and we get the following at the next step.

क्री+ण्+अन्ति

While dealing with this derivation, the fallibility of the C-process and complexity of DOI/SOI operation becomes crystal clear.

32. उद्+विज्+ त (Present, third person, plural)

उद्विज्+त — After deciding आत्मनेपद, परस्मैपद, etc. endings and subsequent application of विकरण by virtue of स्यतासि लृलुटोः (3.1.33), we get the following at the next step:

उद्विज्+स्य+त — At this step, the following sūtras are applicable:

- टित आत्मनेपदानां टेरे (3.4.79), which is पर sūtra with respect to 1.2.2 and पूर्व with respect to others applicable and नित्य sūtra.
- पुगन्तलघूपधस्य च (7.3.86), which is पर with respect to other sūtras.
- आर्धधातुकस्येड् वलादेः (7.2.35), which is पर sūtra with respect to 1.2.2 and 3.4.79 and नित्य sūtra.
- विज् इट् (1.2.2), which is पूर्व and अपवाद sūtra.

1.2.2 blocks operation of 7.3.86 on application of नित्य sūtra 7.2.35. Subsequently, 3.4.79 is applied and we get the following at the next step.

उद्विज+इ+स्य+ते

33. भि+झि (Present, third-person, plural)

भि+झि — जुहोत्यादिभ्यः श्लु (2.4.75) teaches duplication of भि. This, being पर sūtra with respect to sūtra teaching अङ्ग sañjñā, will precede.

भि भि+झि — At this step, duplicated form भि acquires अभ्यास् sañjñā by sūtra पूर्वोऽभ्यासः (6.1.4) and भि भि acquires अभ्यस्त sañjñā by sūtra उभे अभ्यस्तम् (6.1.5), while यस्मात् प्रत्ययविधिस्तदादि प्रत्ययेऽङ्गम् (1.4.13) makes अङ्ग sañjñā. By sūtra सार्वधातुकमपित (1.2.4), झि becomes ङित्. All these sūtras are नित्य, but sūtras 6.1.4 and 6.1.5 are अन्तरङ्ग. 6.1.5, being पर with respect to 6.1.4, entails operation of अभ्यस्त sañjñā sūtra अदभ्यस्तात् (7.1.4). Sūtra 7.1.4, being अपवाद with respect to other sūtras operationalized by अङ्ग sañjñā, will precede, hence we get the following at the next step.

भि भि+अति

34. णिज्+तिप् (Aorist, third person, singular)

णिज् — At this step, णो नः (6.1.63), being पर and अन्तरङ्ग sūtra, is applicable first followed by लुङ् (3.2.110). It is to be kept in mind that 6.1.63 teaches substitution of न् for the initial ण् of the verbal roots in the धातुपाठ and sūtra 3.2.110 teaches affixing luṅ pratyaya in the sense of past tense after dhātu. Besides, sūtra भूवादयोः धातवः first ascribe dhātu sañjñā to √णिज् which entails operation of sūtras 6.1.63 and 3.2.110.

निज्+तिप — Subsequently, after deciding about

आत्मनेपद, परसमैपद, etc. endings, stated step is arrived. At this step, विकरण sūtra च्लेः सिच् (3.1.44) is applied followed by नित्य sūtra इतश्च (3.4.100). However, निषेध option taught by sūtra इरतो वा (3.1.57) first becomes applicable and we get the following at the next step.

निज्+स+त् At this step, the following sūtras become applicable:

i. लुङ्लङ्लृङ्क्ष्वडुदात्तः (6.4.71), the पूर्व and नित्य sūtra

ii. वदव्रजहलन्तस्याचः (7.2.3), the अपवाद sūtra that blocks the operation of पुगन्तलघूपधस्य च (7.3.84) and सिचि वृद्धिः परस्मैपदेषु (7.2.1).

Sūtra 7.3.84 is पूर्व with respect to 7.3.96 and पर with respect to others. Sūtra 7.2.1 is अपवाद with respect to 7.3.84 and sūtra 7.2.3 is अपवाद with respect to 7.2.1.

अस्तिसिचोऽपृक्ते (7.3.96) is पर and नित्य sūtra.

We arrive at the next step:

अ+नैज्+स+ई+त

Should we follow the option other than निषेध taught by sūtra 3.1.57, it will become applicable and substitute अङ् by blocking sutra 3.1.44. Now we get the following at the next step.

निज्+अङ्+त	At this step, अङ् being ङित् blocks operation by sūtra 7.3.84, while नित्य sūtra 6.4.71 becomes applicable and we get the following at next step:

अ+निज्+अ+त्

35. षिच्+तिप् (Aorist, third person, singular)

It is to be noted that षिच् is उभयपदी dhātu, but C-process has taken up derivation in परस्मैपद; hence we are also taking up परस्मैपद form.

सिच्	The derivation is similar to that of example 4. We get the following at the next step:
सिच्+तिप्	At this step, अपवाद sūtra लिपिसिचिह्वश्च (3.1.53) will block च्लेः सिच् (3.1.44) and after application of नित्य sūtra इतश्च (3.4.100), we arrive at the following step:
सिच्+अङ्+त्	Steps are similar to those of निज्+अङ्+त् stated in the example 34.

36. वनु+त्त्वा

वन्+त्त्वा	Sūtra उदितो वा (7.2.56) is अपवाद with respect to नित्य sūtra आर्धधातुकस्येड् वलादेः (7.2.35). निषेध option, being stronger, is applied first and इट् is not augmented. We get the following at the next step:
वन्+त्त्वा	At this step, पर sūtra अनुदात्तोपदेशवनतितनोत्यादीनामनिनासिक लोपो झलि क्ङिति (6.4.37) will block

operation of पूर्व sūtra अनुनासिकस्य क्विझलोः क्ङिति (6.4.15). We will get the following at the next step:

व+त्वा

In the case of non-निषेध (prohibition) option, नित्य sūtra 7.2.35 will be applicable and this will block the operation of पूर्व and पर sūtras 6.4.15 and 6.4.37 respectively. We arrive at the following step:

वन्+इ+त्वा

37. आ+हन्+इट् (विधिलिङ् or Optative , first person, singular, also called potential)

By sūtra आङो यमहनः (1.3.28) हन dhātu prefixed with आङ् is treated here to follow आत्मनेपद endings.

आहन्+इट् At this step, on application of विकरण sūtra कर्तरि शप् (3.1.68), अपवाद sūtra अदिप्रभृतिभ्यः शपः (2.4.72) will elide शप् vikaraṇa. Subsequently नित्य sūtras लिङः सियुट् (3.4.102) and इटोऽत् (3.4.106) are applicable. 3.4.102 is पूर्व with respect to 3.4.106. We arrive at the following:

आहन्+सीयुट्+अत् After applying इत् sañjñā sūtras we will have modified form at next step. It is to be noted that इट् (अत्) is ङित् by virtue of sūtra सार्वधातुकमपित (1.2.4).

आहन्+सीय्+अ At this step, sūtras लिङः सलोपोऽनन्तस्य (7.2.79) and गमहनजनखनघसां लोपः

	क्ङित्यनङि (6.4.98) are applicable. Both the sūtras are नित्य, while 6.4.98 is पूर्व sūtra and 7.2.79 is पर sūtra. We will get the following at the next step
आह् न्+ईय्+अ	At this step, by virtue of ह्+न् , sūtra हो हन्तेर्ञ्णिन्नेषु (7.3.54) will become applicable and we get the following:
आघ् न्+ईय्+अ	

38. व्यध्+क्त्वा

व्यध्+त्वा	At this step, sūtra 6.1.16 ग्रहिज्यावयिव्यधिवष्टिविचतिवृश्चतिपृच्छतिभृतिभृज्जतीनां ङिति च (6.1.16) is applicable, but न सम्प्रसारणे सम्प्रसारणम् (6.1.36) teaches सम्प्रसारण of य and we get the following at next step:
व् इ अ ध्+त्वा	By सम्प्रसारणच्च (6.1.104) we get the following at next step:
विध्+त्वा	At this step, झषस्तथोर्धोऽधः (8.2.40) is applicable and we get the following at the next step:
विध्+ध्वा	At this step, झलां जश् झशि (8.4.52) becomes applicable and we get the following at the next step:
विद्+ध्वा	

39. चल+तिप् (Simple future, third-person, singular)

चल+तिप्	स्यतासि लृलुटोः (3.1.33), being अपवाद to कर्तरि शप् (3.1.68), is applicable after blocking 3.1.68 and we arrive at the following:

चल्+स्य+ति

40. वद्+मिप् (लोट् or imperative, first-person, singular)

वद्+मिप् At this step, कर्तरि शप् (3.1.68), being विकरण sūtra, will be applicable after decididng personal endings, i.e. आत्मनेपद, परस्मैपद, etc. Subsequently नित्य sūtras मेर्निः (3.4.89) and आडुत्तमस्य पिच्च (3.4.92) are applicable. Of these two sūtras, 3.4.92 is पर sūtra and 3.4.89 is पूर्व sūtra and will be applied accordingly. We will get the following at the next step:

वद्+शप्+आट्+नि

41. तृ+तिप् (Present, third person, singular)

तृ + तिप् Readers have already become acquainted with the derivational process, hence here, we are avoiding a detailed discussion.

After application of विकरण, etc. we arrive at the following:

तृ+शप्+तिप् At this step, यण, इत् and गुण processes take place by virtue of sūtras इको यणचि (6.1.74), ॠत इद्धातोः and (7.1.100) सार्वधातुकार्धधातुकयोः (7.2.84). Due to परत्व, 7.2.84 is applicable.

Chapter - 7

Why C-process in Complete Disarray in Understanding Sūtras: षत्वतुकोरसिद्धः (6.1.83), पूर्वत्रासिद्धम् (8.2.1) and असिद्धवदत्राभात् (6.4.22)

Although the above cited three sūtras have been discussed principally in detail above, yet for more clarification with examples, the same are taken up here again.

I. षत्वतुकोरसिद्धः (6.1.86)

Maharishi Dayanand in Vedāṅga Prakāśa, Sandhi Viśaya defines this sūtra as "जो षत्व और तुक् विधि के करने में पूर्व पर के स्थान में एकादेश है, वह सिद्ध कार्य करने में असिद्ध हो जाता है।"

In Prathmāvṛitti, Pt. Bhagvaddutt ji defines this sūtra as "षत्व और तुक विधि करने में एकादेश [असिद्ध] असिद्ध होता है, अर्थात् सिद्ध समान कार्य नहीं होता है। एकादेश को मानकर कोई कार्य प्राप्त हो रहा हो वह न हो, तथा स्थानी को मानकर जो कार्य प्राप्त नहीं हो रहा है वह हो जावे, यही असिद्धत्व विधान का प्रयोजन है।"

Both the definitions imply that in the case of षत्व विधि and तुक् विधि, the single-replacement (एकादेश) in place of पूर्व (preceding) and पर (succeeding) item is deemed as if unknown to carry out सिद्ध (known) operation. It means that the operation does not take place as known. Operation teaching एकादेश, which is desired to take place, does not take place, whereas operation which cannot take place on स्थानी (substituted one) will take place.

Let us understand this by the examples cited below:

Example: 1

किम्+सु+असिचत्	By sūtra किमःकः (7.2.103) we arrive at next step:
क+सु +असिचत्	By sūtra ससजुषो रुः (8.2.66) we get the following at the next step:
क +रु + असिचत्	At this step, by sūtra अतो रोरप्लुतादप्लुते (6.1.109) next step is arrived.
क उ+असिचत्	At this step, by sūtra आद् गुणः (6.1.84) we have the next step:
को+असिचत्	Sūtra एङः पदान्तादति (6.1.105) teaches पूर्व एकादेश and we have the next step:
कोसिचत्	(Note: Modern Grammarians, viz. Grammarians since last 1000 years have started to denote this form as कोऽसिचत्).
	At this step, due to आदेशप्रत्ययोः (8.3.59), ष् is desired in place of स्. However, due to sūtra 6.1.86, this sūtra is treated as असिद्ध (unknown).

This is आदेश-लक्षण प्रतिषेध process.

Example: 2

अधि इण् क्त्वा	At this step, by virtue of sūtra अकः सवर्णे दीर्घः (6.1.97) we arrive at the next step:
अधी+त्त्वा	by virtue of sūtra समासेऽनञ्पूर्वे क्त्वो ल्यप् (7.1.37), we arrive at the next step:

अधी+ल्यप् After इत् operation, we arrive at the next step:

अधी+य Here तुक् आगम् (augment) by virtue of sūtra ह्रस्वस्य पिति कृति तुक् (6.1.69) is not possible due to absence of ह्रस्व vowel. However, by virtue of sūtra 6.1.83, दीर्घ एकादेश operation will be treated like असिद्ध (unknown), thereby entailing the invisibility of long vowel ई 'ī'. So, the short इ 'i' alone will be visible.

अधि + य Now by स्थानिवत् principle and due to visibility of इ, sūtra 6.1.96 will become operative. Subsequently, we will have the next form

अधीत्य

This is the example of स्थानी लक्षण कार्य.

Example: 3

Similarly in derivation of प्र+इण्, the गुण एकादेश operation in place of (अ+इ) by sūtra आद् गुणः (6.1.84) is treated like असिद्ध (unknown) and we are able to derive प्रेत्य, the final form.

The exception to rule 6.1.83 and proof of the failure of the C-process.

Let us review derivation of वृक्षे+छत्रम्, here वृक्षे is in locative case, i.e. सप्तमी विभक्ति.

वृक्ष+ङि+छत्रम् ङि is locative suffix which is affixed to वृक्ष and after इत् of ङ, we arrive at the following:

वृक्ष+इ+छत्रम्	At this step, by virtue of आद् गुणः (6.1.84) we will have following:
वृक्षे+छत्रम्	Now, operation of गुण एकादेश in place of (अ+इ) taught by 6.1.83 will be treated like असिद्ध (unknown) paving way for the application of sūtra छे च (6.1.71) and we will have (नित्य आगम्) compulsory tuk augment.
	However, vārttika "वा सम्प्रसारणङीड्सु सिद्धः" teaches एकादेश, taught due to सम्प्रसारण, ङी विभक्ति and इट् in the matter of षत्व and तुक् augment, is treated like सिद्ध (known).
	In view of the aforementioned vārttika, sūtra दीर्घात् पदान्ताद् वा (6.1.73) becomes applicable, and we have two forms at the next step:

वृक्षेच्छत्रम् and वृक्षे छत्रम्

Similarly, in derivation of शकहूष (शक+ह्वेञ्+क्विप्) due to क्विप् pratyaya सम्प्रसारण एकादेश is taught by sūtra सम्प्रसारणाच्च (6.1.104). Had it been considered असिद्ध (unknown) by sūtra 6.1.83 then 'ष' could not have substituted 'स' by virtue of sūtras इण्कोः (8.3.57) and आदेशप्रत्यययोः (8.3.59).

(शक+ह्व+क्विप् = शक+ ह् उ ए + ०+सु)

In light of the above-stated examples and exceptional cases, it is evident that C-process has limited exposure. Hence, it turned to be verbose while expounding upon the concept of śāstrāsiddhi (unknown rule) and kāryāsiddhi (unknown opertion) and glossed over exceptional cases.

The above exposition makes it easy to understand the applicability of sūtra 6.1.83 and the futility of long-drawn conclusions of the C-process.

II. पूर्वत्रासिद्धम् (8.2.1)

Maharshi Dayanand defines this sūtra as:

"जो कार्य यहाँ से पूर्व सपादसप्ताऽध्यायी अर्थात् एक पाद और सात अध्याय में जितना शब्दकार्य कहा है, वहाँ सर्वत्र त्रिपादी का किया कार्य असिद्ध माना जावे और त्रिपादि में भी पूर्व के प्रति पर-पर सूत्र का कार्य असिद्ध माना जाये।"

This implies that operations taught by sūtras after 8.2.1 will be treated as असिद्ध (unknown) with respect to operations taught by sūtras before 8.2.1. Besides, operations taught by subsequent sūtras will be treated as असिद्ध (unknown) with respect to prior sūtras after sūtra 8.2.1.

C-process has worked with the following examples:

1. राजन्+भिस्

नालोपः प्रातिपदिकान्तस्य (8.2.7) teaches elision of final 'n' and we have next step:

राज+भिस्

At this step, by virtue of अतो भिस् ऐस् (7.1.9), we may have राजैः, but 8.2.1 teaches that लोपः of 'न' will be treated like असिद्ध (unknown). Thus, we will have the following form:

राजभिः

2. अस्मै+उद्धार

In this example, by virtue of

एचोऽयवायावः (6.1.75), we arrive at the following:

अस्माय्+उद्धार

At this step, लोपः शाकल्यस्य (8.3.19) teaches elision of 'y' and we will have

अस्मा+उद्धार

Here if we do not consider sūtra 8.3.19 as असिद्ध (unknown) to आद् गुणः (6.1.84), then गुण operation will occur and we would have wrong form, i.e. अस्मोद्धार instead of correct form अस्मा उद्धार.

3. भुज्+क्ता

In this example, by virtue of sūtra चोः कुः (8.2..30), we have the next step:

भुग्+त

At this step, by virtue of sūtra ओदितश्च (8.2.45), we arrive at the next step:

भुग्नः

Here, both sūtras are under the jurisdiction of 8.2.1, and hence first sūtra 8.2.30 applies, followed by 8.2.45.

4. दह्+तुमुन्

In this example, दादेर्धातोर्घः (8.2.32) is applies, and we arrive at the next step:

दघ्+तुम्

At this step, झषस्तथोर्धोऽधः (8.2.40) will apply, and we arrive at the next step:

दघ्+धुम्

At this step, झलां जश् झशि (8.4.52) will apply and we get the following form:

दग्धुम्

During the course of dealing with these examples, C-process makes the following supposition:

1. While teaching 8.2.1 पूर्वत्रासिद्धम् and 6.4.22 असिद्धवदत्राभात्, Pāṇini has given instructions vis-à-vis DOI but not vis-à-vis SOI. In other words, 8.2.1 and 6.4.22 have no impact on SOI.

2. In the case of SOI, when two rules are operative, then a more specific rule wins, irrespective of the fact that whether it falls under the ambit of sūtra 8.2.1 and 6.4.1.

3. Hence in the derivational example of दह्+तुमुन् sūtra 8.2.32 wins against sūtra हो ढः (8.2.31) by virtue of being specific.

Although the rebuttal of above suppositions have already been provided principally, yet the veracity of C-process is going to be tested hereunder with the help of some examples:

Exception: 1

ओव्रश्चू+क्त = व्रश्च्+क्त

At this step, by virtue of ग्रहिज्यावयिव्यधिवष्टिविचतिवृश्चतिपृच्छतिभृज्जतीनां ङिति च (6.1.16), we get

वृश्च्+त

At this step, the following sūtras are applicable:

- ओदितश्च (8.2.45) is applicable on त of क्त pratyaya.
- व्रश्चभ्रस्जसृजमृजयजराजभ्राजच्छशां षः (8.2.36) is applicable

on च् of वृश्च् dhātu

- चो कुः (8.2.30) is applicable on च् of वृश्च् dhātu
- स्कोसंयोगाद्योरन्ते च (8.2.29) is applicable on श् of वृश्च् dhātu.

In line with C-process assumptions, sūtra 8.2.45 is in DOI relation with other sūtras; therefore, other sūtras, by virtue of sūtra 8.2.1, do not acknowledge the outcome of 8.2.45. Hence, we will have to apply sūtras 8.2.36, 8.2.30 and 8.2.29 prior to the application of sūtra 8.2.45.

8.2.29 is not blocked by applications of 8.2.30 and 8.2.36; hence it will always be applicable.

However, going forward, according to C-process premises, 8.2.36, being more specific than 8.2.30, will apply, whereas 8.2.30 will be discarded.

On following the above-stated logic of C-process, we will get वृष्+न

At this step, by virtue of रषाभ्यां नो णः समानपदे (8.4.1) we will have final form वृष्णः

But this is not the desired form and thus vulnerability of the premises of the C-process is exposed vis-à-vis Ārṣa-vidhi.

Now let us look at how Ārṣa-vidhi solves this mysterious outcome.

Commenting on vārttika: "निष्ठादेशः षत्वस्वरप्रत्ययेड्विधिषु सिद्धो वक्तव्यः" Maharshi Dayanand says, "जो निष्ठासंज्ञाक प्रत्यय के स्थान में आदेश होते हैं; वे षत्व, स्वर, प्रत्यय और इड्विधि के करने में सिद्ध मानने चाहियें।"

It implies that replacement (आदेश) taught in place of निष्ठासंज्ञाक (niṣṭhā-named) pratyayas are treated as सिद्ध

(कलदैल) to perform षत्व, स्वर, pratyaya and इट् processes.

Now by virtue of this vārttika, operation taught by sūtra ओदितश्च (8.2.45) will be treated as सिद्ध (known) to perform षत्व. Hence, this vārttika restricts the application of sūtra 8.2.36 and sūtra 8.2.30 becomes applicable. Thus, we arrive at the next step:

वृक्+न

Now by applying अट्कुप्वाङ्नुम्व्यवायेऽपि (8.4.2) we will have the final form as:

वृक्णः This is the correct form.

Exception: 2 (हरिवो मेदिनं त्वाः - ऋ.खि.पा-10.12.1)

We will here discuss the derivation of हरिवो by following the C-process.

हरि+मतुप्

At this step, by virtue of sūtra छन्दसीर (8.2.15), we have the following at the next step:

हरि+वत्

Now in vocative case (संबोधन), we get the following at the next step:

हरि+वत्+सु

At this step, by virtue of sūtras उगिदचां सर्वनामस्थानेऽधातोः (7.1.70), हल्ङ्याब्भ्यो दीर्घात् सुतिस्यपृक्तं हल् (6.1.66), we arrive at the following form:

हरिवन्त्

Now at this step, when we read this

form with मेदिनं, we will have the following at next step:

हरिवन्त् मेदिनं

At this step, by virtue of sūtras संयोगान्तस्य लोपः (8.2.23) we will get

हरिवन् मेदिनं

By virtue of मतुवसो रु सम्बुद्धौ छन्दसि (8.3.1), we will arrive at the following:

हरिवरु मेदिनं

By virtue of sūtra हशि च (6.1.114), हरिवरु will become हरिवु as follows:

हरिवु मेदिनं

However, by virtue of sūtra 8.2.1, the application of sūtra 8.2.23 is to be treated as असिद्ध (unknown) to sūtra 6.1.114. Thus, the final 'त' of हरिवन्त् will not be elided and derivation of हरिवु by मतुवसो रु सम्बुद्धौ छन्दसि (8.3.1) becomes impossible.

C-process is found helpless in this situation, and, thus, its limitation in understanding the Pāṇinian mechanism is exposed again.

However, vārttika "संयोगान्तलोपो रोरुत्वे" resolves this impasse. Maharshi Dayanand defines this vārttika as "यहां रु को उकारादेश करने में संयोगान्तलोप सिद्ध माना जाता है।"

It implies that संयोगान्तलोप by sūtra 8.2.23 is treated as सिद्ध (known) to sūtra 6.1.114 while doing उकारादेश of रु.

Therefore, by virtue of this vārttika, we are able to derive हरिवो.

Below stated two vārttikas also defy C-process:

* सिज्लोप एकादेशे सिद्धो वक्तव्यः

* संयोगादिलोपः संयोगान्तलोपे

Since, at points no. 21 and 23, chapter 4, we have already discussed these vārttikas, hence, here we are not dealing with them.

III. असिद्धवदत्राभात् (6.4.22)

Maharshi Dayanand defines this sūtra as below:

"इस सूत्र से लेकर इस पाद की समाप्ति पर्यन्त एक प्रयोग में दो समानाश्रय कार्य्य प्राप्त हों, तो पर कार्य्य को असिद्ध मानकर पूर्व विहित कार्य हो जावे।"

Pandit Brahmadutt Jigyasu defines this sūtra as below:

"आभात् यहाँ "आङ्" अभिविधि में हैं अतः आभात् से भस्य (6.4.129) का अधिकार जहाँ तक जाता है, अर्थात् पाद की समाप्ति पर्यन्त ऐसा अर्थ होगा (6.4.175)....... [आभात्] भस्य के अधिकार पर्यन्त, अर्थात् इस अध्याय की समाप्ति पर्यन्त (अत्र)-समानाश्रय अर्थात् एक ही निमित्त होने पर आभीय कार्य [असिद्धवत्] सिद्ध के समान नही होता, अर्थात् आभीय कार्य के होने पर भी वह न होने जैसा इस सूत्र से माना जाता है। 'अत्र' का ग्रहण यहाँ समानाश्रयत्व द्योतन के लिए है। समान-एक ही आश्रय=निमित्त है जिसका, वह (कार्य) समानाश्रय हुआ।"

From both the aforementioned statements following points are perfectly clear:

- ❖ Cause of action or place of action should be common.
- ❖ The adhikāra of this sūtra goes up to 6.4.175.

However, C-process expresses its disagreement with the above observation and provides alternative reasoning which is based on neo-orientalist and occidentalist scholars' works:

- Ancient Indian tradition failed to understand the meaning of असिद्धवत्, आभात् and अत्र in sūtra 6.4.22.
- Adhikara of sūtra 6.4.22 does not extend up to sūtra 6.4.175. Instead, it extends up to 6.4.129.
- Interpretation of समानाश्रय is disputable and not supported by derivational example.

In continuation of the above, the thesis dares Indian Ṛṣis' acumen based on the following derivational examples:

1. हन+सिप् (Imperative, second person, singular)

We have already discussed the derivation of this vide example 14, आख्यातिक section, chapter 6. The relevant point to be noted here is that both sūtras हन्तेर्जः (6.4.36), teaching replacement of हन् with ज, and अतो हेः (6.4.105), teaching (लुक्) elision of हि in the presence of ज, have prakṛti as common āśraya (cause or place of action) and both fall within the ambit of 6.4.22, so the operation of 6.4.36 will be deemed as unknown, so the operation taught by 6.4.105 will not take place, and we will get the form जहि, where हि is not be elided.

2. भू+तस् (लिट् or Perfect, third person, dual)

We have already discussed the derivation of भू+तिप् (लिट् लकार), under "Ārṣa-vidhi", chapter 5. Hence the same does not require any discussion here.

3. शस्+सिप (Imperative, second-person, singular)

In example no. 13 under आख्यातिक section, the derivational process has already been discussed. In this example शस् is the समानाश्रय (common cause or place of action); hence the operation of sūtra 6.4.22 is applicable here. As such, the operation of sūtra 6.4.101 will be unknown and the operation taught by 6.4.35 will take place.

4. पा+लिट् (Vedic perfect participle)

पा+लिट्	At this step, by virtue of अपवाद sūtra क्वसुश्च (3.2.107), we get the following at the next step:
पा+वस्	Here it is to be noted that by sūtra कृत्तद्धितसमासाश्च (1.2.46), प्रातिपादिक sañjñā is assigned to पा+वस्, whereas due to स्थानावित् process, पर and नित्य sūtra लिटि धातोरनभ्यासस्य (6.1.8) is applicable. Since operation of sūtra 6.1.8 is अन्तरङ्ग with respect to operations entailed by प्रातिपादिक sañjñā, therefore sūtra 6.1.8 is to be applied first along with other अभ्यास् sañjñā sūtras, since they are also अन्तरङ्ग with respect to 1.2.46.
प पा+वस्	Now by virtue of sūtra 1.2.46, स्वोजसमौट्छष्टाभ्याम्भिस्ङेभ्याम्भ्यस्ङसिभ्याम्भ्यस्ङसोसाम्ड्योस्सुप् (4.1.2) becomes applicable and we arrive at next step:
प पा+वस्+शस्	Now due to भ sañjñā of शस्, वसोः सम्प्रसारणम् (6.4.131) becomes applicable and we arrive at next step:
प पा+उ अस्+शस्	Since क्वसु is कित् and it has now become अजादि आर्धधातुक्; hence sūtra आतो लोप इटि च (6.4.64) becomes applicable at पा dhātu.
	After the application of सम्प्रसारणाच्च

(6.1.104) and completing इत् process, we arrive at the next step:

प प+उस्+अस्

Above, we have provided derivation by the Ārṣa-vidhi. However, if the derivational steps of the C-process are analysed, then the following colossal mistakes are noted:

1. It reaches पा+वस+शस् step, without assigning प्रातिपादिक sañjñā to पा+वस्

2. It did not complete the process of duplication entailed by sūtra 6.1.8, which is अन्तरङ्ग to sūtra वसोः सम्प्रसारणम् (6.4.131). Therefore, it was forced to apply additional sūtra द्विर्वचनेऽचि (1.1.58) to arrive at desired form.

3. In order to decide which sūtra out of 6.4.64 and 6.1.8 is to be applied first, it is forced to build up a hypothetical case which is devoid of any rationale.

4. It hypothetically considered operation entail by शस् on वस् by virtue of sūtra 6.4.131 and by वस् on पा by virtue of sūtra 6.4.64 to fall within the ambit of sūtra 6.4.22. This assumption is contrary to the concept of समानाश्रय because here cause of action or place of action is not common.

C-process has a similarly built-up case for his hypothesis by irrationally applying derivational steps while deriving पशु+सन्+विट्.

5. प्र+शम् (णिजन्त or प्रेरणार्थक or Causative)

Derivational steps as per Ārṣa-vidhi

प्र+शम् By sūtra हेतुमति च (3.1.26) णिच् pratyaya is suffixed.

प्र+शम्+णिच्	By जनिजृषक्नसुरञ्जोऽमनाश्च, शम् is assigned मित् sañjñā. After इत् process we arrive at next step:
प्र+शम्+इ	By पर and नित्य sūtra अत उपधायाः (7.2.116), we arrive at the next equation:
प्र+शाम्+इ	At this step, मितां ह्रस्व (6.4.92) becomes applicable. It is to be noted that here anuvṛtti of णौ from sūtra 6.4.90, उपधायाः from sūtra 6.4.89 and अङ्गस्य from sūtra 6.4.1 reaches at sūtra 6.4.92. We have the next step:
प्र+शम्+इ	After completion of अन्तरङ्ग process due to णिच्, dhātu sañjñā by sūtra सनाद्यन्ता धातवः (3.1.32) entails operation by sūtra समानकर्तृकयोः पूर्वकाले (3.4.21) and क्त्वा pratyaya is suffixed. We have the next step:
प्र+शम्+इ+क्त्वा	By sūtra समासेऽनञ्पूर्वे क्त्वो ल्यप् (7.1.37), next step is reached as follows:
प्र+शम्+इ+ल्यप्	At this step, due to आर्धधातुक sañjñā of ल्यप्, णेरनिटि (6.4.51) and due to लघुपूर्वात् condition of शम्, ल्यपि लघुपूर्वात् (6.4.56) are applicable. 6.4.56 being अपवाद to sūtra 6.4.51 becomes applicable. We have the next step:
प्र+शम्+अय्+य	

On analysing derivational steps, in addition to errors pointed out for derivational steps at पा+लिट्, example 4 of this section, the following mistakes are evident:

i. ल्यप् pratyaya is replacement (आदेश) for क्त्वा pratyaya. Hence following the principle of स्थानिवत्, ल्यप् will entail operation of sūtra अत उपधायाः (7.2.116). However, C-process indulged in a long-drawn conclusion by ignoring the aforementioned fact and unnecessarily started treating sūtra 6.4.92 and 6.4.56 under the realm of sūtra 6.4.22, ignoring the fact that the place of action in both cases is not common. Sūtra 6.4.92 operates on शम् whereas sūtra 6.4.56 operates on णिच्, hence the condition of समानाश्रय is not fulfilled.

ii. Due to the preconceived notion of proving the concept of समानाश्रय ineffective, C-process ignored the application of sūtra 6.4.51, resulting in the misinterpretation of vārttika.

We are here presenting two more derivations, apart from the derivations discussed above, with the purpose of clarifying more on समानाश्रय concept:

i. अस्+हि	अस् dhātu is read in अदादिगण and for the sake of brevity, we are not going to discuss initial derivational steps. We have started our discussion from the stated derivational form. At this step by पर and अपवाद sūtra घ्वसोरेद्धावभ्यासलोपश्च (6.4.119), we arrive at the following:
अ ए+हि	Now by नित्य sūtra श्नसोरल्लोपः (6.4.111), we get the following at the next step
ए+हि	At this step, due to the presence of 'ए' before 'हि', the operation taught by हुझल्भ्यो हेर्धिः (6.4.101) which is पूर्व sūtra is blocked by sūtra 6.4.119. But

as both 6.4.119 and 6.4.101 fall under the ambit of sūtra 6.4.22 and have common āśraya, i.e. cause and place of action, operation by para sūtra 6.4.119 will be deemed as unknown, so 6.4.101 will see अस्+हि and not अ ए+हि, so it will complete its operation and we will have the following at the next step:

ए+धि

ii. आङ्+गम्+लोट्

आङ्+गम्+शप्+सिप् At this step, by sūtra बहुलं छन्दसि (2.4.73), we have the following at the next step:

आ+गम्+सिप् By नित्य sūtra सेर्ह्यपिच्च (3.4.87), we get the following at the next step:

आ+गम्+हि By अनुदात्तोपदेशवनतितनोत्यादीनामनुनासिक लोपो झलि क्ङिति (6.4.37), we reach the next step:

आ+ग+हि At this step, sūtra 6.4.105 becomes applicable, but since sūtra 6.4.37 and 6.4.105 fall under the ambit of 6.4.22 and they have समानाश्रय, i.e. common cause and place of operation; hence operation done by 6.4.37 will be deemed unknown and 6.4.105 will see आ+गम्+हि and not आ+ग+हि, so, will not be applicable and we will have the following form:

आगहि

Let us demystify the enigma woven by the C-process with regard to the extent of अधिकार of sūtra 6.4.22. C-process' point of contention is that the ambit of sūtra 6.4.22 is up to 6.4.129. Does this premise hold true against Ārṣa-vidhi that अधिकार of 6.4.22 extends up to 6.4.175, as explained above?

We are working with two derivational examples to prove the veracity of Ārṣa-vidhi proposition:

i. सौरी बलाका (सूर्येण एकदिक्)

सूर्य	By sūtra तेनैकदिक् (4.3.112) we have the following at the next step:
सूर्य+अण्	By पर sūtra तद्धितेष्वचामादेः (7.2.117), we have the following at the next step
सौर्य+अण्	At this step, नित्य sūtra यस्येति च (6.4.148) becomes applicable and we get the following:
सौर्य्+अ	At this step, by sūtra टिड्ढाणञ्द्वयसज्दघ्नञ्मात्रच्तयप्ठक्ठञ्कञ्क्वरपः (4.1.15), we get the following:
सौर्य+ङिप्	
सौर्य+ई	At this step, two sūtras become applicable on सौर्य by virtue of presence of ई ▪ यस्येति च (6.4.148): By this sūtra लोप of अ of सौर्य is achieved. ▪ सूर्यतिष्यागस्त्यमत्सयानां य उपधायाः (6.4.149): By this sūtra लोप of penultimate य् of सौर्य is achieved.

If we abide by the C-process' conceptual hypothesis

that the ambit of 6.4.22 is up to 6.4.129, then we are faced with SOI derivational form.

If we apply sūtra 6.4.149, then sūtra 6.4.148 is applicable at the next step. If we apply sūtra 6.4.148, then sūtra 6.4.149 is not applicable at next step due unavailability of penultimate य्. Thus sūtra 6.4.148 blocks the application of sūtra 6.4.149 and is, therefore, more specific. Therefore, by C-process, we will have सौर्यी; but this is not the desired form; hence C-process' presumptions utterly fails.

Ārṣa-vidhi states that अधिकार of sūtra 6.4.22 extends up to 6.4.175. Hence by Ārṣa-vidhi, sūtra 6.4.148 and 6.4.149 falls under the ambit of sūtra 6.4.22, so both sūtras will apply. First, we apply पर sūtra 6.4.149 and then we apply sūtra 6.4.148 and we have desired form सौरी.

ii. गार्गी (गार्ग्याः पुत्रीः- गार्गी की पुत्री)

गर्ग	By sūtra गर्गादिभ्यो यञ् (4.1.105) we have:
गर्ग+यञ्	By पर sūtra तद्धितेष्वचामादेः (7.2.117) we have:
गार्ग+य	At this step, नित्य sūtra यस्येति च (6.4.148) becomes applicable and we will have the following at the next step:
गार्ग्+य	
गार्ग्य	At this step, by यञश्च (4.1.16) we have:
गार्ग्य+ङीप् or गार्ग्य+ई	At this step, two sūtras यस्येति च (6.4.148) and sūtra हलस्तद्धितस्य (6.4.150) becomes applicable.

If we follow C-process, then it is a case of SOI. Here again, we are stuck because due to ई, sūtra 6.4.150 and 6.4.148 are applicable on गार्ग्य. Similar to the above example, 6.4.148 being more specific, will block the operation of sūtra 6.4.150. This will result in a wrong derivational form: **गार्ग्यी.**

The derivational step of traditional Ārṣa-vidhi resolves this deadlock as it treats both the sūtras: 6.4.148 and 6.4.150 under the ambit of sūtra 6.4.122.

6.4.150 being पर sūtra is applied first followed by sūtra 6.4.148 and we have गार्गी which is the correct form.

Chapter - 8
Competition between Paribhāṣās (Metarules)

C-process in Appendix A and Appendix B has explored the applicability of the following sūtras:

अलोऽन्त्यस्य (१।१।५१)

ङिच्च (१।१।५२)

आदेः परस्य (१।१।५३)

अनेकाल्शित् सर्वस्य (१।१।५४)

तस्मिन्निति निदिष्टे पूर्वस्य (१।१।६५)and

तस्मादित्युत्तरस्य (१।१।६६)

C-process here, too, keeping with its disposition, mocked the acumen of Indian Ṛṣis and refused to accept the rationale of Ārṣa-vidhi.

Before probing into the C-process, it is better to discuss Paribhāṣā-61 of Pāribhāṣika by Maharshi Dayanand, along with relevant derivational examples.

Paribhāṣā-61 states "उभयनिर्देशे विप्रतिषेधात् पञ्चमीनिर्देशः।"

Maharshi Dayanand explains this paribhāṣā as "जहां सप्तमि पञ्चमी दोनों विभक्तियों से निर्देश किया है, वहां (तस्मिन्निति०; तस्मादित्यु०) इन दोनों सूत्रों में परविप्रतिषेध मान के पञ्चमीनिर्दिष्ट का कार्य होना चाहिये।"

It implies that where an operation is governed by ablative and locative case, then considering the applicability of पर sūtra, operation by ablative case gains precedence.

Let us understand this Paribhāṣā through the derivation of भूमा.

बहु It is read in पृथ्वादिभ्य गण; hence by sūtra पृथ्वादिभ्य इमनिज् वा (5.1.121) इमनिच् pratyaya is suffixed to बहु.

बहु+इमनिच् At this step, sūtra बहोर्लोपो भू च बहोः (6.4.158) is applicable.

Let us first do the पदच्छेद of this sūtra.

बहोः (5.1), लोपः (1.1) भू (लुप्त प्रथमान्तनिर्देशः), च (अव्यय) बहोः (6.1)

Now let us analyse the anuvṛttis extending to this sūtra:

इष्ठेमेयस्सु (7.3) from sūtra 6.4.154,

भस्य (6.1) from sūtra 6.4.129

अङ्गस्य(6.1) from sūtra 6.4.1.

On closure analysis, it is observed that बहु is in ablative (पञ्चमी) case while इष्ठन्, इमनिच् and ईयसुन् are in locative (सप्तमी) case. Now a question arises whether लोप is to be applied at इष्ठन्, इमनिच् or ईयसुन् which follows बहु or is to be applied at बहु, which precedes इष्ठन्, इमनिच् or ईयसुन्?

This dilemma is resolved by Paribhāṣā-61 and accordingly by sūtra तस्मादित्युत्तरस्य (१।१।६६) लोप is applicable at the pratyaya इमनिच्.

But now the question is at which part of pratyaya, लोप is to be applied?

	To answer this, sūtra आदेः परस्य (१।१।५३), which is complementary to sūtra 1.1.66, states that it is to be applied at the first sound, i.e., इ of इमनिच् pratyaya.
	Accordingly, we get the following at next step:
भू+मन्	At this step, by sūtra अनेकाल्शित् सर्वस्य (१।१।५४), भू replaces बहु.

Similarly in the derivation of आस्+शानच् (आन्), by sūtra ईदासः (7.2.83) ईत् is to be applied. In sūtra 7.2.83, there is anuvṛtti of आने from sūtra 7.3.82 and अधिकार of अङ्गस्य from sūtra 6.4.1. आसः of sūtra 7.2.83 is in ablative case, आने is in locative case. In accordance with the paribhāṣā-61 ईत् is to be applied at आ of आन् and we will have आस्+ईन् at the next step.

Based on *Paṭhan Pāṭhana ki Anubhūt Saralatama Vidhi* and *Prathamā* Vṛtti, let us have a look at Pt. Brahmdutt Jigyasu's exposition on following sūtras.

1. अलोऽन्त्यस्य (१।१।५१), (अलः ६।१॥ अन्त्यस्य ६।१॥)—जहां षष्ठी-निर्दिष्ट के स्थान में आदेश कहें, वहां वह अन्त्य अल् के स्थान में हो।

It implies that replacement, if taught in the genitive case, takes place at the final letter.

2. ङिच्च (१।१।५२), (ङित् १।१॥ च अ०)—ङित् आदेश भी अन्त्य के स्थान में हो। **यह सूत्र अनेकालशित् सर्वस्य (1.1.54) का अपवाद है।**

It implies that ङित् substitution replaces the final letter. This sūtra is अपवाद to 1.1.54.

3. आदेः परस्य (१।१।५३)—(आदेः ६।१॥ परस्य ६।१॥)—जो पर अर्थात् उत्तर को कार्य कहें, वह उसके आदि अक्षर को हो। **यह सूत्र तस्मादित्युत्तरस्य (१।१।६६) का शेष है तथा अलोऽन्त्यस्य**(१।१।५१)का अपवाद

है।

It implies that replacement, administered for 'para' (following) item should be affected at the first letter of the following item. This sūtra is complementary to sūtra 1.1.66 and is अपवाद to sūtra 1.1.51,

4. **अनेकाल्शित् सर्वस्य** (१।१।५४), (अनेकाल् १।१॥ शित् १।१॥ सर्वस्य ६।१॥) — अनेकाल् और शित् आदेश सब के स्थान में हो। यह सूत्र **अलोऽन्त्यस्य** (१।१।५१) का अपवाद है।

It implies that replacement consisting of multiple sounds or whose श is इत् takes the place of all letters or sounds.

5. **तस्मिन्निति निदिष्टे पूर्वस्य** (१।१।६५) — 'तस्मिन् इति' = सप्तमी विभक्ति से निर्दिष्ट किया (पढ़ा) हुआ जो शब्द हो, उससे पूर्व जो शब्द या वर्ण हो, उसी को कार्य । अर्थात् उससे परे और व्यवधानवाले को न हो।

Operation stated in the locative case (सप्तमी) applies to the letter immediately preceding it unintervened.

6. **तस्मादित्युत्तरस्य** (१।१।६६) — जो पञ्चमी विभक्ति से निर्देश किया कार्य है, वह व्यवधानरहित उत्तर के स्थान में हो। **'आदेः परस्य'** सूत्र इस सूत्र का शेष है।

Operation stated in the ablative case applies to the item immediately following it unintervened.

C-process expresses its disagreement with the above conclusions on the following grounds:

- There is no evidence in the wording of आदेः परस्य 1.1.53 or elsewhere to suggest that the presence of an ablative form in an operational rule constitutes a necessary condition for the application of 1.1.53. So, 1.1.53 governs any para or right-hand side (RHS) operation.

- Since Pāṇini has specifically taught 1.1.53 for RHS substitutions, he has likely taught both अलोऽन्तस्य (1.1.51) and ङिच्च (1.1.52) only for LHS substitutions. I agree with the tradition on the scope of अनेकाल्शित् सर्वस्य (1.1.54), I think that Pāṇini has taught 1.1.54 for both LHS and RHS substitution.

To establish the veracity of its hypothesis, C-process relies upon लोट्, third person, singular form of लिख् dhātu. लिख् dhātu falls under तुदादि गण, hence by virtue of sūtra तुदादिभ्यः शः, we will have शः pratyaya in place of शप् vikaraṇa, but C-process, inadvertently worked with शप् pratyaya. However, we have taken the correct form in the derivational step.

लिख्+श+तु

At this stage C-process while discussing application of sūtra तुह्योस्तातङाशिष्यन्यतरस्याम् (7.1.35) proposes as under:

- The only rules that can potentially govern 7.1.35 are 1.1.53 and 1.154. Since 1.1.55 has been specifically taught for substitutes made up of multiple sounds, it is more specific than 1.1.53. Therefore, by 1.1.54, तु is entirely replaced with तातङ्, giving the correct form लिखतात्.

C-process, on the strength of its above-stated assumptions, rejects vārttika of Kātyāyana on sūtra 7.1.35.

At point no 33, chapter no. 4, we have already discussed the anomaly of the C-process' assumption. In the light of Maharshi Dayanand's exposition on

Mahābhāṣya, it is apparent that sūtra 1.1.54 is applicable in the present example.

In the light of Paribhāṣā-61, in the example of भूमा and explanation of Maharshi Dayanand at point no. 33, it is evident that Ārṣa-vidhi is the only proper means to understand Maharshi Pāṇini from his perspective.

5. Sūtra दीर्घात् पदान्ताद्वा (6.1.73), आद्यन्तौ टकितौ (1.1.45)

While discussing derivation of सर्वेषाम् and कुटीच्छाया, C-process discarded Indian Ṛṣi's interpretation of sūtra 6.1.73 and 1.1.45. We have already delved into the limitation of the C-process at point no. 32, chapter 4 above.

However, for the benefit of readers and scholars, we reiterate here that sūtra 6.1.73 is to be read in relation to sūtra 6.1.72. In sūtra 6.1.72, there is a discussion about augment of तुक after the long vowel आ and before छ. But sūtra 6.1.73 discusses the insertion of long vowels other than आ. Hence it is अपवाद of sūtra 6.1.72. Therefore, the augment of तुक् has to be attached to the left-hand side of the long vowel, similar to that of आ in sūtra 6.1.72.

Besides, Vārttika: "विश्वजनादीनां छन्दस्युपसंख्यानम्", read at 6.1.73 also supports this assumption and talks of optional augment of तुक् in case of small vowel (ह्रस्व). This vārttika is an extension of sūtra 6.1.73 and an exception (अपवाद) to sūtra 6.1.71.

Examples for sūtra 6.1.72

दीर्घात्= (ह्री+छति = ह्रीच् +छति ह्रीच्छति; म्लेच्छति),

पदान्ताद् वा = (गायत्री+छन्दः = गायत्रीच्+छन्दः = गायत्रीच्छन्दः,

In the absence of तुक-augment, it will be read as गायत्री छन्दः

Example for vārttika “विश्वजनादीनां छन्दस्युपसंख्यानम्”

विश्वजन+छत्रम् = विश्वजनच्+छत्रम् = विश्वजनच्छत्रम्

In absence of तुक-augment it will be read as विश्वजनछत्रम्

Chapter - 9

Why Ārṣa-vidhi, the way forward for Sanskrit Students

Maharshi Dayanand in the third chapter (तृतीय समुल्लास) of the *Satyarth Prakash* advises that those who wish to be intelligent, diligent, virtuous and wants to develop Vedic intellect should continuously learn and teach Aṣṭādhyāyī for one and a half year, thereafter for another one and a half year, one should master Mahābhāṣya. By conforming to this timetable, any one can become an accomplished Vyākaraṇācharya.

Subsequently, after attaining brilliance in Vedic and Laukika Sanskrit lexicons, one can easily master and teach any Vedic scientific works. In comparison to the efforts put in for attaining mastery over Sanskrit Vyākaraṇa, other subjects require little or no effort once excellence has been attained in Sanskrit Vyākaraṇa.

On the contrary, despite putting in gigantic efforts for fifty years in learning disgusting books, viz. सारस्वत, चन्द्रिका, कौमदी, मनोरमा, one can never master Sanskrit Vyākaraṇa, which can be achieved in three years by Ārṣa-vidhi. It is because "**The Great and Respected Maharshis**" have elucidated every subject cogently, which can never be done by lay scholars.

The brief history of revival of Ārṣa-vidhi (Seers' Mechanism) to study Āṣṭādhyāyī in modern times is given below:

Guru Virjanand Dandi Swami (1778-1868) was one of

the leading propagators of Ārṣa-vidhi in modern times and was the teacher to many, including Maharshi Dayanand Saraswati (1824-1893). He was highly critical of Bhaṭṭoji Dixit etc. He used to condemn these scholars with the following statements:

"सूत्रक्रम तोड़कर अध्ययन-मार्ग बिगाड़ने वाले भट्टोजी दीक्षित आदि प्रथम कुत्सित है। उनके ग्रन्थ दूसरे कुत्सित हैं। उन ग्रन्थों के पढ़ने हारे तीसरे कुत्सित हैं। ये तीनों मिलकर कुत्सितत्रय अथवा क्यत्ति कहाते हैं।"

This statement implied that three categories of people and texts are worthy of being castigated:

i. Bhattoji Dixit (1550-1630) etc., who distorted the original sequence of Aṣṭādhyāyī sūtras

ii. Texts composed by these Scholars

iii. Those who read and learnt these texts

Guru Virjanand Dandi Swami used to define Sanskrit Vyākaraṇa as "अष्टाध्यायी महाभाष्ये द्वे व्याकरणपुस्तके, अतोऽन्यत् पुस्तकं यत्तु तत् सर्वं धूर्तचेष्टितम्।।"

That is, only Aṣṭādhyāyī and Mahābhāṣya are two authentic books for learning Vedic and Laukika Sanskrit Vyākraṇa; the rests of the books are works of low-grade scholars.

Pandit Brahmadutt Jigyasu (1892-1964) prescribed Sanskrit curricula in the following sequence:

Prathmāvṛtti (Commentary on Aṣṭādhyāyī) constitutes one third of the curriculum, Paribhāṣā, etc., constitute another one-third and the rest one-third is accomplished by the study of Mahābhāṣya. Of these, Prathmāvṛtti is the main part of Sanskrit Vyākaraṇa.

From the above quoted narration of Guru Virjanand

Dandi Swami, Maharshi Dayanand Saraswati and Pandit Brahmdutt Jigyasu ji, it is apparently evident that the rest other methods except Ārṣa-vidhi are not suitable for learning and teaching Aṣṭādhyāyī. Hence if anyone yearns to learn Sanskrit Vyākraṇa from a proper perspective, Ārṣa-vidhi is the only way out, which is able to pluck out the actual and factual intention of great grammarian Pāṇini.

Finally, before concluding, two more points require clarification:

I. अयज इ इन्द्रम (Example 4, p. 232, Appendix-C of the Thesis): It is a first person form of अयज्+शप्+इ and इन्द्रम् is in the accusative case.

Paribhāṣās 43 and 44 define and resolve the confusion. By पूर्वोपस्थितिकम् अन्तरङ्गम् we obtain this form. Let us understand this by the following example:

- पटु ई आ: Here two यण sandhis are available. One by the interaction of उ+ई and the second by ई+आ. Which of the two is to be applied is resolved by vārttika पूर्वोपस्थितिकम् अन्तरङ्गम् which says that first one, i.e., उ+ई is अन्तरङ्ग and is to be applied first. Hence, we arrive at form पट्व्या. Similarly in case of अयज इ इन्द्रम we arrive at अयजे इन्द्रम.

II. पचाव इदम (लोट्, first person): Here in Vedic usage, sūtra एत ऐ (3.4.93) which is अपवाद to आमेतः (3.4.90) is applicable. But since sūtra 3.4.90 has not been applied, so by virtue of लोटो लङ्वत् (3.4.85), we have the following form:

पच्+शप्+आट्+वस् इदम् instead of पच्+शप्+आट्+वहि इदम्.

पचाव इदम् - Since एकार is not applicable here, so ऐकार is

not required, hence we arrive at the form पचावेदम्.

From the preceding discussion corroborated with examples, it is sufficient to prove the robust mechanism of Ārṣa-vidhi to understand and apply the Pāṇinian derivational machine and bust the false propaganda of claiming to have cracked the 2500-year-old algorithm of Pāṇini. Hope this detailed explanation with evidence will help readers and scholars to understand the Pāṇini from his perspective and importance of Ārṣa-vidhi (method) to learn Sanskrit and Vedic grammar.

www.ingramcontent.com/pod-product-compliance
Lightning Source LLC
Chambersburg PA
CBHW050014170726
48282CB00025B/404